From Average to Excellent

How I Transformed My Dreams Into Goals, Goals Into Plans, and Plans Into Success

Isaiah "Ike" Johnson

Major Retired

To: Kendall
My Grandbaby
Papa love you.
Ike Johnson

From Average to Excellent Copyright © 2021 by Isaiah "Ike" Johnson. All rights reserved. This book or parts thereof may not be reproduced in any form, stored in any retrieval system, or transmitted in any form by any means—electronic, mechanical, photocopy, recording, or otherwise—without prior written permission of the publisher, except as provided by United States of America copyright law or for the use of brief quotations in a book review.

Although the author and publisher have made every effort to ensure that the information in this book was correct at press time, the author and publisher do not assume and hereby disclaim any liability to any party for any loss, damage, or disruption caused by errors or omissions, whether such errors or omissions result from negligence, accident, or any other cause. Views expressed in this publication do not necessarily reflect the views of the publisher.
Printed in the United States of America

First Printing, 2021
ISBN 978-1-941749-83-8
4-P Publishing
Chattanooga, TN 37411

CONTENTS

"I have a very high sense of fairness, justice, and equity because I've seen so much injustice growing up and throughout my life; I have developed a zero-tolerance personal policy for the mistreatment of people anywhere."

Ike Johnson

Introduction

I never dreamed about military service, much less becoming a Marine, but becoming a Marine officer made for an improbable story. But I did it! The path that led me from the farm in New Hebron, Mississippi, to become a Marine officer is nothing short of miraculous. Especially during a time and place that I thought nothing good could and would ever happen to me. There were days growing up I felt I would never leave the farm, much less leave the state of Mississippi. As a black person, I knew about my history of slavery. Growing up on that farm, I felt like a prisoner in my mind, but there was always hope.

Growing up in Mississippi in the 1950s and 60s felt like there was no end in sight to the disappointments, agony, and distress that I witnessed my parents going through. The way of life that I was born into was not a pleasant one. Don't get me wrong; I had wonderful parents. They were God-fearing, kind, and loving people, but they demanded hard work from their children. My father was a farmer, preacher, and pastor. My mother was one of the greatest mothers that the world had ever known. She was a homemaker and the hardest working woman that I had ever seen. If I had to describe my parents' traits, principles, and values they passed on to my nine other siblings and me, I would have to do it this way. My father, Papa, was a leader. He was a reserved and quiet man. However, he was firm, fair-minded, hardworking, and a man of extremely high principles.

Mama was a God-fearing woman. She was a caring and giving person who loved her children and taught us to work hard for what we wanted to accomplish. She would often tell us she enjoyed working and seeing things grow. Mama would say, if a job is worth doing, do it well. If you came to our house, you would leave with; food, a coat, shoes, or something she gave you. I guess I got my father's serious side and my generosity, love, and concern for people from my mother.

My parents were both God-fearing people, and each of us children accepted Christ Jesus early. I accepted Christ when I was five years old, under my mother's teaching. I learned to pray and ask God for what I needed, hoping He would hear me. Things were difficult for me, as I saw it, living on the Mississippi farm. I prayed every day and night that there would be a better life for my family and me one day.

My Parents taught me about Heaven and what a wonderful place it was. I even dreamed about it, but a better life between where I was, and Heaven seemed so far away. I could not understand how to create a better life than how I lived on that farm. I could only dream in my mind's eye of what that might look like, which was extremely limited because most of the people around me were in the same condition. However, I was full of hope. Even though I could not see how things could change in the physical, I dreamed big dreams and set goals for my future that I could not see.

Little did I know that the leadership and training that my parents imparted into me daily was sticking. My parents always encouraged us to tell God what we wanted through prayer, hope, and faith. However, it would not be until I was in my early twenties that I began learning the concept of leadership, dreams, hope, faith, goal setting, and how to mix these things with my prayers and hard work to see things change in my favor. Then I realized this was what my parents had been trying to teach me all the time.

When I understood these concepts, my life began to change. These things have made all the difference in the world to improve my life. As I better understood these concepts, I found myself sharing, mentoring, and teaching them to others who found themselves where I was as a youth or young adult, feeling hopeless, lost, and without some guidance to lead the way. But I had guides, and I did not realize it; they were my parents–Auther and Edna Johnson.

I have great empathy for youth and young adults who find themselves where I thought I was on that proverbial farm in Mississippi. When I hear young people say they can't wait to be grown to change their life situations and make things better for themselves and their families, I listen more intently. That's where I was as a young person growing up in Mississippi with what I thought was no guide to help me understand what was going on. I had not learned to pay attention to what was happening around me. I needed to appreciate what was going on and apply myself where I was at the time.

At twenty years old, the direction that led me into the United States Marine Corps is nothing short of miraculous. To devote almost twenty-seven years of my adult life to be a part of the Marine Corps is amazing to me. In retrospect, I can see how God's hands were guiding me. Especially when I saw where and how the seeds of my entire life were planted. On that dirt farm in South Central Mississippi, I realized that every step of my life was being designed and honed by my parents, siblings, and environment, but God ordered those steps. Everything changed for me when I learned to set goals, achieve them, and plan for the curveballs ahead because they were coming. It is life!

I am convinced that we are all guided in similar ways by this unseen hand. The force behind my life story and your story may have the same ingredient at the starting point. But when we have parents, a guide, a coach, and a mentor, we become more of who we are designed to be. In life, we are often presented with two directions; two roads to choose; our choices make all the differences in our lives. Joining the United States Marine Corps was a turning point in my life and turned out to be one of the best decisions that I have made.

Looking back, I feel that the first twenty years of my life were a setup for the next forty-five years and beyond. I hope that I have made the best of them with the opportunities that I have been afforded: as a leader, mentor, life coach, spiritual leader, deacon, teacher, trainer, and life guide, husband, son, brother, father, grandfather, and hopefully great grandfather one day. I have enjoyed every gift given, every opportunity and challenge that life has presented. I don't know how many people I have influenced or impacted along the way. However, I know that I've benefited from others. I hope that I have been equally generous to others with my time, talents, and treasures.

Over time, I've gotten a little feedback from a few people I have known and met along the way. Most of them, I feel, have been a bit too generous with their praise of me because I'm the debtor to them all. However, many of them have excelled and surpassed the feeble efforts or support I may have provided for them. Isn't that what life is supposed to be about; people helping people and the student exceeding the teacher?

When people asked what I attribute to my success, I smile in amazement and say, "Let's see how my generation speaks about me." I want to leave behind a life of hard work and faithful service because that's all that I know. I hope this book encourages, motivates, and inspires you to trust your true self, live your best life, and leave your mark that makes someone else better than themselves.

Isaiah "Ike" Johnson

Leadership Style Development

Before entering the United States Marine Corps, I saw myself as a leader and a pretty good one. I survived nineteen years of farm experience with nine other siblings and two authoritarian parents who knew what was best for me without asking my opinion. I observed leadership displayed with my parent's setting goals, managing a 120-acre farm, and raising ten children. However, this authoritarian style was not one that I preferred. I had to develop some leadership skills and styles to combat and survive in this environment. I tried to find my role of influence and leadership in the family. I only had two subordinates, my two young brothers.

From the beginning of my Marine Corps career, I had no less than twelve people I was responsible for, including their conduct and well-being. This leadership thing became important to me because leaders and leadership were always emphasized in the Marine Corps. Early in my career, I had the opportunity to learn about leadership in a way that began to pique my leadership interest. This experience stirred up some lessons drilled into me early by my parents: honesty, fairness, planning, setting goals, and looking out for others. This leadership course made me think about the type of leader I wanted to be. The Marine Corps taught about the history of the great leaders. They gave us a list of traits, principles, and more specific training on leadership types:

- Delegating
- Participating
- Laissez-faire (let it be)
- Directing

Over time, leadership styles have significantly evolved. I was introduced to leaders and their leadership styles. As I developed my leadership style, I questioned why one leadership style that worked for one didn't work for others. I realized that one specific style used by the leader worked on everyone, but it was not the most effective. In most cases, it had a limited impact on the people they were leading. By the time I became a sergeant, I had attended several formal leadership classes and training. The leaders I observed never varied the use of different styles; they only used one technique to accommodate the people they were trying to influence.

Leadership and mentoring are the game changers in the lives of others. Early in my life and career, I made it my goal to help other people. My dilemma was choosing what leadership style or type I wanted to use to identify myself and my brand. All I knew was that I wanted to be one of the best leaders in the Marine Corps. I had already determined that a single leadership style would not work well for each person because everyone was different. To be most effective, a leader must use the right style and understand the followers' knowledge, ability, and willingness to do the task assigned. I came away from most leadership training experiences understanding that leading differently requires more work on the leader's part. Leaders leaned towards one leadership style because it is easier.

I learned about Situational Leadership from Paul Hersey and Ken Blanchard in a leadership training session in my community. This style offered the best perspective on leadership. I am convinced that this is one of the best ways to influence people to complete any job or task and to improve people at all levels. The Marine Corps provided excellent tools and opportunities to develop my skills to be a successful leader. However, early in my military career, I chose to be a situational/transformational leader because I saw my peers and leaders using one style and getting minimum results. Leadership is challenging work. A leader must work for outstanding results from all parties involved. When leadership is done correctly, the outcomes and rewards are much greater for the organization, the people being led, and the leader. Situational leadership theory refers to those leaders who adopt different leadership styles according to the situation and the development level of their team members. It is an effective way of leadership because it adapts to the team's needs and sets a beneficial balance for the entire organization. The situational leadership approach uses four leadership styles:

- Telling
- Selling
- Participating
- Delegating

The leader selects the appropriate style according to the situation and the readiness level of the followers.

Since my retirement from the Marine Corps, although my uniform has changed, my commitment to being a situational leader and helping people has grown stronger. I've been spending my time and effort trying to influence people to be a better form of themselves to have a better quality of life and help better those lives around them. I see this as our mandate and gift to our fellow man, woman, and the universe. Helping as many people as possible to reach their calling, dreams, and goals in life is my mission statement.

Goal Setting as a Key to Success

I also share my story hoping that you may be encouraged, inspired, and motivated to build on to your life and make it better in some small way. If you are stuck socially, spiritually, economically, lack proper education and training, or maybe you have just been knocked down by some recent setback, I say to you—You Can Make It! You can get up and move on because it is better at the next level! It is awesome at the "top," and that is where I will see you. The top is where you should see yourself next week, next year, and in five years and beyond. Through prayer, tell God what you want. Know that He wants to help you achieve your dreams and goals if you set them and create a plan for them. Then, go to work and watch them happen for you.

I do not know why you have taken the time and effort to read this book but let me say that I am grateful that you did. Perhaps you are like I was during the first twenty years of my life, trying to make my life better without any goals, plans, or direction. I was trying to figure out where I fit into this game called life without proper mentoring and guidance but struggling and hoping for a better day.

I want you to know that despite everything, there is a place for you. Let me assure you that you are more than capable of the journey ahead. With hard work in the direction of your purpose, you can "Do, Be and Have" anything that you set your mind to do. By thinking, dreaming, planning, believing with faith, trusting, and continuing to think, "As a man thinketh so is, he." You are what you think about. Let me prove this to you now. Think about a blue car, and today you will see all the blue cars in your path. The blue cars have always been there, but today you are thinking about blue cars. I promise you that you will see them.

We do not know where we are going because we think about things that we don't want to happen and do not focus on what we want. Focusing on what I wanted to happen for me liberated me from the shortcomings and short-sightedness that plagued my earlier thinking. I thought about my dreams in a negative sense. I could not see them succeeding. I only thought about all the reasons why they wouldn't come true, so I made no plans for their accomplishment. When I began making plans and setting goals and objectives to accomplish my tasks, I set timelines for their success. I began to believe that my dream was possible.

Before I knew it, I was having the success I wanted to see. I trusted God to help me. I wrote my plans down and read them aloud to myself daily. This made all the difference in the world for me. "Faith without works is dead." I thought it was the old farm in Mississippi's fault that I was unsuccessful. I thought it was poverty or because I was lacking. I thought it was my lack of the right friends and family member's fault. I even thought it was because of the color of my skin. These things may have had some influences, but nope, it was none of these things in totality.

I will tell you what it was as you continue to read, but here is a hint; it was me and my stinking thinking. It was the limited vision I had of myself; not knowing what I had inside of me was truly enough. All the time, I just needed people in my life to help me activate what was inside.

For you who are reading this because you can identify with my message, thank you. For those of you reading and know someone who needs to hear this message, please pass it on. If you have crossed my path, I say thank you for helping to make me who I am. I am grateful to you. Let's take our dreams and set some S.M.A.R.T. goals and change and improve our lives! More about that later. I learned to believe in long-range planning. Long-range planning and goal setting help keep you focused on what you want. It keeps away negative distractions. I believe in sharing my goals with people with like minds.

Keep saying what you are going to do often and every day. This is to remind yourself more than reminding others. Tell them what you plan to "do, be and have" with your support group. Write it down. Look at what you've written and always keep it in front of you. Don't let it out of your mind. Here are just a few goals that I set along life's voyage:

- Play college basketball
- Earn a college degree
- Become a Marine officer
- Teach for high school and college
- Create a mentoring organization for youth and young adults
- Run for public office to represent the people around me

Did I accomplish each of my goals? You will have to keep reading to discover the answer to that question!

Family and Farm

I am from a small farming town in South-Central Mississippi called New Hebron. My hometown is in Lawrence County, but I lived in Simpson County, where Mendenhall is the central town. I was born on October 11, 1952. My parent's names were Auther Johnson and Edna Mae Moore Johnson (both deceased). I am the twelfth child of fourteen children born to their union. The first three babies were stillborn or dead at birth. The fourth child was born alive but died shortly after birth.

My parents named me Isaac. However, the midwife, Aunt Peale Lena Johnson (not related), wrote the name Isaiah on my birth certificate. For the first nineteen years of my life, I was known as Isaac. Even now when I visit home, I'm known as Isaac, even to my siblings. I discovered my name was Isaiah when I received my official birth certificate to join the United States Marine Corps. What a shock! However, I learned to live with the name change and moved on. I have seven older siblings and two younger ones. My family was comprised of twelve people: my parents, three girls, and seven boys.

In 1938 or so, my mother and father were married and bought a piece of property from a man we called Uncle Dick; he was not our uncle by blood, but that's what we called him. He sold my parents 120 acres of some of the worse land in the community. I'm told that people in the community were taking bets that my parents would not be able to keep the land, much less turn it into a farm. The land was primarily wooded when they purchased it. My father and mother were hard-working people. They proceeded to clear the land with their bare hands and made a home and a farm for the ten children they birthed and raised on that hollow grown.

My oldest brother, born in 1940, was named Auther Jr. (deceased at 73 years old). Auther Jr. was the first child that lived. We called him Bubba. After Auther Jr., my parents had nine more children over the next fifteen years. My oldest sister, Mary, was born in 1942; she was affectionally known as Sweetie. Next was Ernestine (Shug), born in 1943, then Eddie Mae (Eddie) in 1945. I think she was my father's favorite. She is the one that could get Papa to change his mind most of the time when it pertained to her not doing something. Eddie was named after our paternal grandfather, Ed Johnson.

After three girls in a row, there came six boys.

Robert Herbert (Hubert) was born in 1947. He was often called the seventh son. I don't know why, but he was the luckiest person in the family growing up. In 1949 Rossco (Rock) was born. He was the smart guy in the family. I am told he went from the first grade to the fourth grade in one week. Rossco read all the books they had in the elementary class. He graduated high school at age sixteen. Andrew (Pete) was born in 1950. Then there was me, Isaac. I was born in 1952. My brother Woodrow (Woody) was born in 1954. Finally, the baby of the family, Moses, was born in 1955. Reverend Moses followed in our father's footsteps; he is the pastor and preacher of the family. These are the twelve individuals I lived with that shaped my thinking and development in my early years. The other major factor in our lives was our faith in God. The Oak Ridge Missionary Baptist Church and the surrounding community helped to make us who we are today.

I remember my older brothers and sisters working on the farm, picking cotton, pulling corn, feeding the animals, milking the cows, riding the mules and horse, and doing the chores around the farm. We had a lot of animals for food, work, and play on a farm that size. As a little boy, I could not wait until I was old enough to work with my older brothers in the field. It looked like they were having so much fun. It was the cotton-picking season before my fifth birthday, and I had been begging Papa to let me go to the field. I guess I wore him down by telling him how badly I wanted to go to the field and work with him and my siblings. One fateful day, my mother made a cotton sack for me from a twenty-five-pound cloth flour sack. I can remember like yesterday.

Papa asked, "Isaac, are you ready to go to the field?"

I said, "Yes, sir, I am."

He took me to the cotton field with him. I worked alongside him all afternoon. I filled my sack with cotton. He said he was so proud of me, and he gave me a quarter. The following day, as my brothers and sisters were getting ready to go to the field, I was still in bed as usual. I heard Papa calling my name.

"Isaac, are you ready to go?"

This was the end of my innocence and life of no work as I had known it. I worked on the farm until I was seventeen years old, plowing mules, picking cotton, pulling corn, planting, nurturing. We harvested vegetables, cucumbers, and anything that would grow, and we could eat, sell, or give to someone. We grew most of what we ate. That was the beauty of the farm and farm ownership. Some families in our community were still sharecropping during that time.

They lived on white-owned farms and worked for those families. My father was an only child with a half-brother and one-half sister. My mother had a large family of fifteen brothers and sisters, and most of them had ten children and owned their own farm. A few years later, I got put into the lineup of taking turns slopping the hogs, milking the cows, and sharing in all that fun that I thought my older brothers and sisters were having. My life was never the same.

Education Through Life Observation

I was excited to finally start first grade in 1958. Mrs. Jewel Walker was my teacher. She also attended the same church I attended, which was not good. Not that I was a bad child, it was just that she would always give my parents updates on me each week. This did not take long to get used to because this would be my life, along with my siblings, for the next twelve years. We all grew up in each other's shadows. My father was one of the local preachers and pastors. There was no one in the community or the surrounding area that did not know the Johnson family.

My Parents, Auther & Edna Johnson

The Early Days of Life on the Farm

I was about five years old when my mother told me the story of my birth into this world on October 11, 1952. I was born on a Saturday night weighing eight pounds and four ounces. There was no hospital for childbirth for African American families living in the rural counties in central Mississippi. A midwife delivered me. The Saturday that I was born, our neighbors who lived on a farm next to us, an African American family, had a baby girl a few minutes after midnight that Sunday morning. Her name was Willie Mae.

In the early years after our birth until about age seven, we celebrated our birthdays together. Whatever cake our mothers baked, we shared with each other. Everyone on both sides of our families thought that something would come of that relationship. But after we started school and met new people, that thought vanished. Willie Mae got a double promotion from the first grade to the second grade, so she graduated a year ahead of me. I don't know how that happened. I felt that I was just as smart as she was, but she moved ahead of me. This was the first time I began to have questions about the fairness of life, personal influences on people, and situations. I figured who you know is how you succeed?

We never had much money, but we did not go hungry. My mother was a terrific cook, and my sisters learned most of her cooking skills and still carry them forward. I know because I can still gain at least five pounds without thinking about it when I go back home to Mississippi. My sisters have my mother's hospitality spirit; you must eat something when visiting their homes.

Our kitchen was one of the largest rooms in the house, filled with a long wooden table with twelve chairs. It was always a busy place. Until about 1960, the old wooden stove is how my mother prepared meals in the early days. The woodstove was also used for heating bathwater. When I was about ten years old, we modernized and transitioned to a gas stove. I ate most of my meals as a family around that table. Everyone in the family sat down to three meals each day, and you had to be on time.

We raised chickens and hogs on our farm which was our main source of meat. We slaughtered two to three hogs each year during the winter. My father and older siblings would all play a part in this wonderful ritual of hog killing. We would salt the meat and store it in the smokehouse. Mama and my sisters would clean the chitterlings and make hogshead cheese, pork shoulders, bacon, and sausage. These were all products of the hog. Mama would make our version of Crisco© shortening by frying the fat from the hog's belly, which produced lard (shortening). Occasionally, we slaughtered a cow. This was a big deal. Beef! We are talking about steaks. We considered this "eating high on the hog," as the old saying goes. Everything on the farm was useful in one way or the other. If you did not eat it, we sold it for profit.

My father loved to fish, and we went fishing in our spare time. My father always brought home buffalo fish when he went fishing. The buffalo fish is famous in the South. It is so boney that my older brother and sister would remove the bones before the younger children could eat.

Growing up, my parents had a creed or rules by which we lived. They did not call it that, but they had a saying they tried to ingrain in our thinking thru repetition. Love God; work hard; take care of each other; do your best at everything that you do, treat others the way you like to be treated; and God will take care of the rest.

I learned essential things about achieving success. My parents wanted us all to go to school and get a good education. Still, I could not put my ideas together because there was always something happening in our family life or community that would devastate my thinking, dim my hopes, and set back my belief system. I knew that living as a farmer's family was not something I would have picked for myself; it was handed to me. I had to figure out how to create a better life for myself, so I did what my mother and father told me to do and focused on getting the best education I could from our segregated school in Simpson County. I was blessed with many supportive and encouraging teachers and opportunities that did not come to every student in the South's poor rural area during that time. In the ninth grade, my math teacher, Mr. Clayton, nurtured my love of math and instilled the confidence in me to achieve and solve my problems.

People told me I'd never get off the farm. They said I'd live there until I got old, and my teeth fell out. They reminded me that I didn't have the background of smart people in my family to succeed. Well, I may not have been intelligent about some things about farming, but Mr. Bob McNair, my agriculture teacher, was a great source of inspiration. My father would try to spark the entrepreneurial spirit in each of us by giving us a pig to raise so we could sell it and use the money as we wanted. Or he would provide us with a spot of ground and let us grow our small crop alongside the family crop. Whatever the crop made, we could have the money from it. This also fell in line with Mr. Bob McNair's program. As the agriculture teacher, he would come to our farm and check our project, recognizing those with the best livestock or crop. Those experiences left me with a sense of pride and accomplishment in learning to take responsibility and knowing that I could accomplish and produce something as an individual. After I got married with kids, whenever we traveled across the country, I would point out something about the farm when we saw one. Even today, I am appreciative and grateful for the opportunities and lessons that my parents and teachers taught. They have sustained me throughout my life.

My father was a man among men. He had an absentee father but, somehow, he managed to raise ten wonderful children with the help of my mother by his side. Life for a black family farmer in the 1940s, '50s, and '60s in central Mississippi was challenging because of the physical labor required. We had little machinery and did most of the work with mules and horses. We did at least have a home to live in, a one-hundred-and-twenty-acre farm, and a farmhouse with no bathroom or running water until I was about ten years old. We had to rely on the outhouse located in the backyard. The outhouse was a simple wooden shed with a hole dug in the ground with a wooden frame built around it with inside seats. We had a two-sitter. We often couldn't afford toilet paper, so we would make sure there was an ample supply of old newspapers and magazines. Sometimes corn cobs were used to clean oneself. Our house had a tin roof. I recall many rainy nights lying in my bed, listening to the rain hitting the roof, and thinking, *everyone else in the world cannot be living like this. There has got to be something better out there.*

A Country Boy's Dreams and Nightmares

Thinking about the phrase, it takes a village; we had that village where I grew up. I could do something at school or in the community, and before I got home, my parents knew about it. I completed my twelve years of school without too much fanfare. I played JV basketball in the seventh and eighth grades. However, I did not make the high school basketball team. I guess it was because everybody was good at basketball in my community, and there were only so many slots. I always dreamed of playing basketball at the college level, but I could not make the high school team. I do not know where that dream came from, but I could not shake it. This dream became a reality for me when I turned it into a goal. I played college basketball because I made it a goal to keep working on my basketball skills at every opportunity. I knew that it would happen for me if I kept playing basketball and learning about the game.

Homelife was difficult on the farm, mentally and physically. We always had food, but sometimes we barely had what we needed in other things. Sometimes, I felt we were rich, depending on how well the crops that year. But Mama and Papa always provided what we needed. My mother would can food in quart jars and store them for the winter months. During harvest time, we would miss school for thirty days because we had to gather the crops. There were times the crop did not turn out so well, and we would go to the Delta. The Delta is a place in north Mississippi where we picked cotton to make up for the losses. Sometimes, in these situations, we would sharecrop with a white farmer to make things work out for that season. Our principal, Mr. Gray, and our teachers would work with us with our schoolwork. Papa would go to school and get our assignments; we would complete them at night. At some point, Papa would return them to our teachers before the week or grading period was over. That is how we kept up when we had to miss school for the harvest. Every morning before I went to school, I had chores to do. I would milk one or two cows, feed the hogs and chickens, and my brothers did the same. We all had tasks to do in the morning before school.

One morning I was running late for school. The time for the bus to arrive was getting close. I had the additional chore to draw water from the well because it was Mama's wash day. I was running out of time. My brother Andrew and I had a cow to milk every morning. My Mama knew precisely how much milk to expect from the cows each morning, so I tried to negotiate with him for some of his milk, so I could have milk to bring in without milking my cow. Andrew would not help me this day. So, I went into action. I quickly milked my cow and got half the milk I would typically get and added water for the difference. I caught the bus at 7:15 that morning, right on time.

I felt good about what I had done and how brilliant I thought I had been that morning. I did not account for the chemical reaction of fresh milk; the cream rising to the top after it set for an hour or so. That afternoon when I got home, my mother was waiting for me because the cream, which would be used to make butter, did not rise on my milk. I learned a couple of life lessons that day. First, do not take shortcuts. Secondly, that cream will rise to the top of the milk and the top of the class. Along with my life lessons, I got the whipping of my life when I got home from school that day. Most severe incidents on the farm by us children were always followed by corporal punishment, which I thought was terrible. In retrospect, I never made the same mistake twice. Do not get me wrong. This was not child abuse. It was always done lovingly. My mother would always have a teaching moment before she whipped you. My father's teaching moments were to the point, so I preferred my father's discipline. Sometimes, my parents would say, "This will hurt me more than it will you." I would think, please give it to yourself (only my deep thoughts). When I became a parent, I understood precisely what they were saying to us. Our way of life on the farm was one of trust. We had to trust each other. Our parents had to trust us to do what we were supposed to do because there were enough enemies outside. Jim Crow Laws were the biggest enemy of our time. My parents taught us to do what we were supposed to do when we were supposed to do it, or there were consequences.

I learned valuable lessons on the farm. My brothers and sisters dubbed me the laziest person on the farm. I always remind them that I always got my work done, and they never did it for me. They said that about me because I always thought I had a better idea or a smarter way of doing things. I always presented my father with more innovative ways to do something. Papa didn't always agree with my philosophy, but I tried to sell him on it anyway. He'd say, "Boy, you are lazy." Raising as many boys as my parents did in the South during that time had to be a mother's nightmare; trying to keep her black boys alive and getting them to manhood was a challenge for any black parent back then.

Ironically, the same phenomenon is happening today, some fifty years later. When we left home, my parents would give us a behavior lecture on how to behave when interacting with white folks. “Make sure you say yes sir, no sir, yes ma’am, and no ma’am; be respectful, and you should not have any problems.” This worked most of the time. However, there were times when it didn’t because there were always some white folks who wanted to make you the target of their fun, exercising their privileges under the Jim Crow Laws of separate but equal. There was nothing equal about anything where I grew up in the ’50s and ’60s. Fortunately, I had six brothers and three sisters. We rolled deep. If you saw one of us, there were two or more close by.

Occasionally, we would have what I call run-ins with white people who did not know us. Hubert and Rossco were in town one day and bought a tire for the truck. Before they got back home, the tire had gone flat. Hulbert and Rossco returned to the store and explained to the man what happened. The shop owner, in no uncertain terms, told them, "Nigger get out!" Hubert would not leave without the tire. Rossco tried to get him to leave and fight another day, but you must know my brother Hubert; he persisted for his new tire. The shop owner got his shotgun and threatened to shoot him. That did not phase Hubert at all. Hubert said, "If you shoot me, you are still going to give me a new tire." The store owner gave Hubert the tire. I've had many encounters with racism while growing up in Mississippi.

Our farm was located about a three-quarters of a mile off the main highway. You would know you were coming to our house because we were the only owner who lived down that road. However, our mailbox was on the main highway. One day, I took my brother's motorcycle and went to get the mail. After getting the mail, I noticed a car was approaching me quickly. These were the types of situations that your parents tried to prepare you for if you found yourself alone with hostile white folks. I crossed the highway, started down my road to the house, but the car advanced and ran me off the road into the ditch. By the time I could get my wits about me, three white men were standing all over me, one with a gun pointed in my face. I was about twelve years old.

The man with the gun said, "Nigger you better stop when you see the law."

They were not in a police car, but one has a sheriff's badge on his uniform.

They continued, "Whose boy, are you?"

I told him who I was. They began looking as if I was the wrong Nigger, because they knew who my father was. Then they looked at the old scooter that I was riding and wrote me a ticket for no tag. They let me go with tears in my eyes and with the ticket in my hand. I returned home and told my mom what happened. She said, as she always did in these matters, wait until your father gets home. When my father got home, I told him what happened, and he told me not to worry. When things like this happened to us, my father would see the individual who did it or see a white person of influence in the community to remind them to pass the word not to mess with his family. My father was highly respected and sometimes feared in the community because he was a minister and because of his father's reputation.

My grandfather Ed Johnson was not a lawful man, but he was ethical. I am told that he had this strong sense of right and wrong. "Eye for an eye" was his creed. If he told you not to do something and promised to shoot you for it, just tell him where you wanted the bullet. Grandpapa Ed was non-discriminatory. He shot White and Black people. I'm told that he spent time in prison for some of his deeds. A story is told that my Grandpapa Ed walked into a general store and told the white owner, "I need some things for my family. I don't have any money now, but we can do this one way or the other. I can shoot you and get what I need, or you can let me have it, and I will come back and pay you for it when I get the money."

The store owner replied, "Ed, take whatever you need."

It was incidents like this that made my grandfather the legend that they say he was. My father never spoke about his father in those terms, but it was people in the community, white and black folks, who had these same stories about my grandfather, Ed. People would tell us that our Grand Papa Ed was a great man. My mother would tell us how kind of a gentleman he was. Grandpapa Ed stayed with my parents off and on for a period before his death. My mother told us that Grandpapa Ed stayed with them until after my older brother, Auther Jr., was born. Grandpapa died in 1942. He was forty-two years old.

The following Saturday morning, my father and I went to see Mr. Little about the ticket. He was the justice of the peace. We walked up to his house.

My father said, "We are going to court, son."

He told me to sit on the porch. Papa went inside for about twenty minutes.

He came out, said, "Let's go."

We got in the truck and were on our way home.

"Papa, where was the court?" I asked.

"We just had it. Mr. Little gave us a break. He only charged us eight dollars. He let the court costs go," he responded.

I was sick to the bottom of my stomach and confused. In my heart of hearts, I felt that those three white men had violated my rights somehow and had broken the law by treating me the way they did. But I did not know what law they violated. The sad thing about it was no one seemed to care but me. Right then and there, I set the goal and vowed that I would go to college and learn the law when I grew up. True to promise, I have a bachelor's degree in Criminal Justice.

Living in the South was challenging if you wanted freedom and equal rights. It was like living in some prison system where all the rules only applied to the black folks, and white people could do what they wanted, even to you. For example, in my little town, we had water fountains for white folks only and water fountains for black folks only. There were restaurants for white folks only. Black folk had to go to the back-door restaurant for service. Before we went to town, my father would tell us to use the bathroom and get a drink of water because he would not let his children humiliate themselves by using any black-only accommodations. I guess it was the perfect form of Jim Crow, separate but unequal. Therefore, a better life was always in my thoughts. It had to be somewhere, but I never thought that Mississippi could change.

Developing and Shaping My Worldview

In 1960, I met my first local hero, a man named John M. Perkins. We would later call him Dr. John Perkins. John was the first type of Dr. Martin Luther King Jr. in our community. John grew up in the same town as I did just in an earlier generation. I was about twelve years old when I first met him and his family. His son Spencer and I were the same age and good friends before they moved twenty miles away to Mendenhall, Mississippi.

In 1960 John moved from California back to Mississippi with his wife Vera Mae and his five children. They moved to my tiny hometown of New Hebron. John and his family became active members of our local church, Oak Ridge Missionary Baptist Church. John got all the church boys together and started what I now call the first mentoring group, The Boys Shepperd League. Each week, John would get us together on a weeknight and teach us Bible and life lessons. The best part was he would have store-bought snacks, which was the highlight of the evening.

I never thought of a man as a friend because all the adults in my life were considered old people. I guess

John was in his early thirties. He was born in 1930. I felt I could relate to him better than any other adult man in our community. John had a unique way of teaching the Bible. He had felt flannels with an easel storyboard. He could make Bible stories come alive. Within a few months, John was coming to my school and doing chapel sessions regularly. He moved on to the local junior college. He evangelized everyone that he could touch. You must understand, my father was a minister too, but John Perkins had a unique way of communicating with the youth of my day.

John's mother died from starvation when he was seven months old. His father abandoned John, so his grandmother and extended family of bootleggers and sharecroppers raised him. John was about seventeen when he moved from Mississippi to California In 1947 to live with other family members. His family was concerned that his life might be in danger because of his brother Clyde's death. Clyde was gunned down in our small town by a police officer.

After joining the Army and serving in the Korean War, John settled in southern California. In 1957 he converted to Christianity after his son Spencer invited him to attend the church he had been going to since he was a little four-year-old boy. John got converted or saved, as we call it, in the Baptist church. John was a disciple and began teaching and preaching all over southern California. John tells the story about how God told him to return to his place of birth, Mississippi, and in 1960 he did just that. This is when I first met Dr. John Myron Perkins. John is one of the few men who left an indelible print on my life. This man helped shape my thinking to know things could be better. But if they are to be better, you must first do something about it yourself, and others will help.

Motivated by a desire to help their neighbors and their own children, John and Vera Mae started a daycare center from their home from 1966 to 1968. It became a historic program in the community's "Head-Start Program." John and Vera Mae started their ministry, "The Voice of Calvary," in Mendenhall, Mississippi. Initially concerned with evangelism and Bible literacy, John had a growing conviction that the gospel of Jesus Christ also addressed spiritual and physical needs.

In one of the poorest counties in Mississippi, John became concerned about the state of Black people in our community. In 1965, Perkins supported voter registration efforts in Simpson County. In 1967, he became involved in school desegregation when he enrolled his son Spencer in the previously all-white

Mendenhall High School. In the fall of 1969, John became the leader of an economic boycott of white-own stores in Mendenhall. On February 7, 1970, following the arrest of students taking part in a protest march in Mendenhall, John was arrested and tortured by white police officers in Brandon, Mississippi, while in jail. Remarkably, John emerged from this terrible experience with a renewed commitment to his vision of a holistic ministry that saw the bondage of racism inflicted on both white and black people and the damage and deprivation it caused in the communities. He summarized his philosophy of Christian ministry in the three Rs, relocate, redistribution, and reconciliation. John Expounded on this philosophy in 1976 in the book "The Quiet Revolution." [1]

I reconnected with John's mentoring in 1992. I was in my car on the Marine Corps Base in Camp Pendleton, California, listening to a gospel radio station when I heard the minister say, "John Perkins says..." He goes on to quote what he said. I pulled my car over. I could not believe what I was hearing. My mind raced back to 1960 when I first met John. My thoughts were, could this be the same Dr. John Perkins who nurtured my thinking as a young boy? That night, I called my

---

[1] John M. Perkins - Wikipedia. https://en.wikipedia.org/wiki/John_M._Perkins

sister Eddie in Mississippi, and asked if she knew where Dr. Perkins was. Eddie told me that he was in Jackson, Mississippi. I told her to tell him that I wanted to speak with him. She said she would.

I reconnected with that giant of a man and have visited with him on several occasions. He still inspires me. I did not realize how much Dr. Perkins affected me growing up until I spent some time with him as an adult. I went to Mississippi for our high school's 45th-anniversary event. I invited him to attend with me. He declined. I reminded him that everyone there would remember who he was and that he has impacted them just like he has influenced me. He finally agreed to go, and he was the life of the party. On our way home, he said to me, "Isaac, I am glad you talked me into going. I could not believe they all still knew who I was, and the personal stories each one of them had about me were amazing."

Dr. John M. Perkins is now ninety years young and still making a difference in people's lives in West Jackson, Mississippi.

My Mentor, Dr. John M. Perkins

My First College Attempt

In August 1969, as I was getting ready to enter my senior year of school, I got the blow of my life. Papa died at age Fifty-two. I was sixteen years old and devastated. My father was the hero of our entire family. He was larger than life to me.

During this time, my older brothers and sisters were grown and had gotten married—the four youngest boys left at home were my brothers Andrew, Woodrow, Moses, and me. When I think about my father's death in retrospect, he tried to prepare my brother Andrew and me for this because we were the oldest at home. The entire year before Papa died, he would take us aside and reemphasize all the aspects of farming and remind us that we would have to carry on one day without him. To which we paid no attention.

That summer, he promised us a trip to New Orleans for two weeks with one of our sisters Earnestine and her husband. My sister Ernestine and her husband picked Andrew and me up that Sunday night. We said our goodbyes to everybody. My father fought back tears as we were leaving; I thought that was strange since I had only seen my father cry one time before, and that was when my brother Hubert went to the Army. Andrew and I went to New Orleans and had a wonderful time. That first week we went to a football game to see the Saints play that Sunday. When we returned to my sister's house that evening, we got the call that my father died. The best I can explain how it felt was like someone hit me in the gut, sucked all the air out of the room, and pulled the floor from under me. Even at the age of 68, I cannot fully explain the feeling. Thank God the hurt has eased, but there isn't a day that goes by that I do not remember my father, his leadership, his strength, and the wisdom that he provided for all of his children.

I graduated in May of 1970 and headed off to college in August. Before my father died, he told my mother to make sure I went to college. To fulfill his wish, I enrolled at Prentiss Institution, a local junior college. It was a two-year college about twenty miles from my hometown. Several of my brothers and sisters had gone there. I started there on a work-study program. Work-study is where you can have any number of jobs at the college to help pay for school costs. These jobs ranged from farm work to janitorial service, milking the cows, and feeding the chickens. Somehow, I got one of the choice jobs in the college work-study program. I was the driver for the college's president, Dr. Johnson. I was Dr. Johnson's driver but, she rarely went anywhere. I remember driving her to the grocery store once. The rest of my time was spent cleaning her garage, flower beds, and whatever else she wanted me to do on Saturdays. I wanted to honor my father's wishes, But I was just not ready for college, so I dropped out after three months.

I tried to explain to my mother why I could not stay in school. This was the most difficult discussion my mother and I ever had in my life. I told her I could not, in good faith, go to college because she could not afford it. She countered by telling me that of all the children in the family, my father wanted me to go to college the most. We talked all night. I left her with a promise that I would get my college degree someday. My mother gave me her blessing to pursue my best self. I was incredibly grateful that she allowed me to do what I felt I needed to do. My ideas were to get a trade and then get a job and have a good life. I knew one thing about my future: college was not a viable option when I graduated from high school

Less than two years later, my mother died. I was nineteen years old, barely getting over my father's death. I was truly in a free fall with my life. One of my primary concerns was not only my grief, but I tried to imagine how my two younger brothers, Woodrow and Moses, felt. I just knew how I was, and I can only imagine how they were processing what was happening in our lives.

After I dropped out of college, I went to live with my brother Robert (aka Herbert) in Fayette, Mississippi, where he ran a Manpower program teaching welding. In three months, I was a certified welder, and my brother Herbert took me and several of the students to the Gulf Coast of Mississippi to get jobs. I went work at the shipyard in Pascagoula, Mississippi, building Navy ships. Within weeks, my supervisor saw my potential and put me in an apprenticeship program to become a supervisor in three years. I had to go to the local junior college every day before work to learn things like blueprint reading, etc. I realized I was still not ready, but I tried it anyway. After three months, I bailed out of the program and moved to New Orleans, Louisiana.

My sister Ernestine and her husband agreed to let me live with them, I got a job in the local shipyard, and all was well. I moved out into my own place with high school buddies and was on my way, I thought. After a few months, I got laid off. This was not the plan. It was tough. I was just trying to make a way for myself and become independent. I tried to stay in Mississippi, but

I knew that employment there and in New Orleans was temporary because, in my mind, I was being called in an entirely different direction. I called my brother-in-law, Staff Sergeant Carlie Davis. He was a United States Marine Corps drill instructor at Parris Island, SC.

My Hero from the Cotton Field

A year prior, my brother Andrew and I had gone to Jackson, MS, to take the military entry test for the Marine Corps because we knew we would be drafted. Neither one of us decided to join. However, a year later, we didn't get drafted. My brother Andrew got married, and for some reason, I felt like this was the time for me to join.

My brother-in-law Carlie Davis is now a retired Marine, Master Gunnery Sergeant E-9. Carlie has retired from the Marine Corps after twenty-six years of honorable service. He is a two-time Vietnam Veteran with two Purple Hearts. Carlie returned home in 1966 from Vietnam after his first tour and married my sister Eddie. I was thirteen years old, but I could not get over those Dress Blues and that this American Hero would help us pick cotton and do farm work just like he was a part of the family. He was influencing me, and I didn't realize it. The fact that I knew someone that went halfway around the world to war, got shot twice, and returned to tell us about it was simply amazing.

Carlie was my image of a Marine's Marine. I was a country boy and had not left Mississippi, but he was the first military hero I had ever known. As I was lamenting and contemplating my next move, I called and had a heart-to-heart talk with Carlie. I asked him if he thought I could make it in the Marine Corps. Without hesitation, he assured me I could make it. On December 1, 1972, I joined the United States Marine Corps. It was one of the biggest and best decisions that I have ever made in my life.

Military Life

Off to Parris Island, SC. Marine Corps Boot Camp

I was sworn into the Marine Corps on November 9, 1972. I volunteered to be an Infantry Marine because it had a $1500 bonus. I started my active-duty time in the United States Marine Corps in December 1972, before Christmas. I wanted to be out of Mississippi before the anniversary date of my mother's death, which had taken place the year prior in December. I took a flight out of New Orleans, reporting to Parris Island, South Carolina.

When every Marine recruit gets off the bus at recruit training, they stand on painted yellow footprints on the ground. At 3:00 in the morning on the 1st of December, I found myself on the yellow footprints with about sixty-five other young Americans. When the drill instructors spoke to us in a manner that I had never experienced before in my life, I started second-guessing my decision to join. Over the next few weeks, I thought a lot about how terrible life was on the farm during the 1950s and 1960s; however, farm work did not compare to what I was going through. I remembered my mother always reminded me that if it's worth having, it's worth the work. I did well in boot camp. I was a squad leader the entire time while there, and I was meritoriously promoted to Private First Class E-2. At graduation, I had a total change of mind. I left Parris Island as a proud United States Marine Corps, Private First Class. Goal completed. I went home to Mississippi for ten days of leave before going to Camp Pendleton in Oceanside, California.

Camp Pendleton California

I reported to Camp Pendleton, California, for Infantry Training School for six weeks. At the end of my training, I didn't realize that I had to qualify as an M60 Machine Gunner to get my $1500 bonus. Lucky for me, I had a great instructor who committed to get me, a left-handed Marine, to qualify on a right-handed M60 machine gun. I was successful, and after six weeks of training, I was assigned the Military Occupational Specialty (MOS) of M60 Machine Gunner. Then I was off to my first duty station, Okinawa, Japan, for one year.

Okinawa, Japan. June 1973

My year in Okinawa was good for me, but I did not like being that far away from home. While stationed there, I went on a six-month deployment on a Navy ship. I was able to see the world of the Far East, Yokosuka, Fuji, Japan, Philippines, Taiwan, Hong Kong, and

South Korea. The time passed quickly, and the year was up before I realized it. I was promoted twice in Okinawa, from Private First Class E-1 to Lance Corporal E-3 and Meritorious Corporal E-4. After Okinawa, I was reassigned to Marine Corps Base Camp Lejeune, NC.

Camp Lejeune, North Carolina 1974

Shortly after I reported into the unit, I was made aware that I was assigned to the unit on a deployment to the Mediterranean Sea for six months. Wow, here I go on to another Navy ship for another six months. I began to think that I had signed up for the Navy because I had spent one year at sea on Navy ships in my first two years in the Marine Corps.

In 1974, after checking into my unit, I met a beautiful woman named Annette Walker. Annette and I met through a friendship between her sister Bertha and her brother-in-law Clarence and my sister Eddie and my brother-in-law Carlie. They had been friends for several years. Both of our sisters were married to military men. Eddie's husband, Carlie, was in the Marine Corps, and Bertha's husband, Clarence, was in the Air Force. I had just returned from Okinawa, Japan, and my sister Eddie and her husband Carlie were moving back to North Carolina from Parris Island,

South Carolina. I was home in Mississippi on vacation but returned to North Carolina a week ahead of them. They told me they left the car with some friends at Camp Lejeune, and I could go by and use it until they returned in a week. Their friends who had the vehicle were Bertha and Clarence, and I was about to meet my wife for the first time.

When I got to Camp Lejeune, I stopped by Bertha and Clarence's house to pick up the car. Bertha told me that her sister, Annette, had gone to work in the car, and I could come back later to get it. I picked up the car later and returned to my base at Camp Geiger. I did not know the car needed a base decal, so I could not drive on base. The next day, I returned to Bertha and Clarence's home, but I needed a ride back to the base. Annette agreed to give me a ride. On the way back, Annette and I made small talk. I asked her if she had a boyfriend, and she said no. I could not resist asking her if she wanted to go to a movie with me sometime. She agreed, and that next night we went to the movies. After the date, we started to hang out a lot. I became highly interested in her as a future partner. When Summer ended, Annette went back to college for her junior year, and I left for a six-month deployment to the Mediterranean Sea on a Navy ship. Annette and I vowed to stay in touch by letters, and at that point, I decided that this would be my future wife. You must understand that I was the only one of the ten siblings who was not married, and I was the last to do so.

While on the deployment, I wrote letters to Anette without a single response. I wrote several more letters, which made me overly concerned about our relationship. I started to second guess myself about her being my future wife. I returned from the six-month deployment in March 1975. I waited for Annette to return to visit her family for the summer because she had some explaining to do. When Annette returned that summer, she swore she had not gotten any of my letters, claiming she thought I had lost interest. After assuaging my feelings, we made up and had a wonderful summer together. I popped the question with the ring in hand. She said yes. Annette graduated college in May 1976. During this time, I had transferred to Parris Island for drill instructor school to become a Marine Drill Instructor.

Back to Parris Island, South Carolina

Annette graduated from Talladega College in Alabama with her bachelor's degree in psychology. We agreed we would wait for two years to get married. Annette graduated and returned home to Havana,

Florida, a small town outside of Tallahassee. After returning home, she found things quite different at her parents' house. She called me one day and said, "Let's get married now." I was a little surprised. However, I asked her to come to Parris Island for a visit. I wanted her to see and understand how challenging this tour of duty would be over the next two years. I explained that the divorce rate for drill instructors was 50% and that those odds were not good for our future marriage. I also explained to her that I would not be home every third night and that I would be leaving at four every morning and getting home somewhere between six and nine in the evening. I wanted her to understand the challenges of being a Marine's wife.

Annette told me none of that mattered, and she could handle it. This was when I knew I had a partner for life. She came to visit for a few days; I gave her the tour of Parris Island. I wanted her to return home and think about it, and she did. To make a long story short, she returned in a week. Annette and I got married in June 1976, in Beaufort, South Carolina, after I graduated from Drill Instructor school. We've been married forty-one years and counting.

Over the next two years, I had several major life events. We bought a mobile home, I was meritoriously promoted to staff sergeant, and we had our first child, Isaac II. All of this within two years while working at one of the most demanding assignments of my career. In October 1977, our son Isaac II was born; I was a proud father, but, unfortunately, I must confess the first year of my son's life was exactly as I described to his mother. The time I spent with him was minimal because being a Marine Drill Instructor consumed my life. The hard work that I put in those two years paid off. After six months, we bought our first home, a mobile home, and put it on base. This made my commute to work shorter and improved the time that I could spend with my family.

I thought about my career in the Marine Corps more seriously. I remembered how I promised my mother that I would get my college degree. Completing a successful two years as a drill instructor allowed me to choose my next duty station. I looked for ways and places to work on my college degree while serving in the Marine Corps. A fellow Marine had left the drill field about a year before my leaving. He had been assigned to the University of North Carolina as Assistant Marine Instructor. He was back at Parris Island with some of his students. I spoke with him in the chow hall and asked how he liked the assignment. He explained to me that it was the best-kept secret in the Marine Corps. I asked if he had time to get a degree.

He looked at me in amazement and said, "I guess you could if you want to." It was evident that he had no interest in getting his degree. I later found that over fifty colleges and universities around the country had jobs for former drill instructors. I spoke with my career planner, and he found a vacancy at the University of Missouri that needed an Assistant Marine instructor.

Time to Set the Goal for a College Degree

It was time to move again. I moved my family from Parris Island to the University of Missouri in Columbia, where I was assigned as the Marine Officer Instructor. I was in pursuit of my goal, a college degree.

The University of Missouri 1978

In June 1978, my wife and my baby boy Isaac relocated to Colombia, Missouri. When I reported, I met and my boss, Major Ingraham. The first thing he told me was, "Ike, drop your pack and grow some hair. You are not on the drill field anymore." We had a small staff at the university. I taught all the basic military courses. Major Ingraham taught the more sophisticated stuff like the Art of War, Surface Warfare, etc. The team of officers and Navy Enlisted Chiefs was great. Our families were close, and we all got along fine. However, the community outside of the university was still stuck in the fifties and sixties.

Part of my job was to be a great ambassador in the community for the Marine Corps and the Naval Reserves Officer Training Corps. I connected with the American Legion and the local VFW, where we coordinated the use of their facility for special functions such as the Navy and Marine Corps Birthday Ball, annual celebrations, and other unit functions. It was not unusual for a senior officer at the unit, a Navy Captain, to say to me, "Gunny, let's take the staff and some senior midshipmen out to the VFW for happy hour on a Friday." I would set it up because I had become well known at the VFW, American Legion, and in the community with the veterans. The gentleman that oversaw the VFW and controlled things had become a good friend. Out of respect for me when I was in the building, he would tell the guys to knock it off when the Nigger word was flying around the room a little too loud and much.

On one occasion, the Navy Captain, the Chiefs, and a few midshipmen were there having happy hour on a Friday afternoon. A couple of old veterans came and sat down with us. We started having conversations and telling war stories. There was one older gentleman who had been in the battle of Okinawa. We had talked before and had many discussions. When I was in the building, it seemed that he enjoyed talking with me. On this day, he shared with the midshipmen about life back in St Louis. Being comfortable with me (maybe a little too comfortable), he mentioned how the Niggers there had messed up the neighborhood park where he was from. After saying this, it felt like a minute of pure silence. He realized I was sitting next to him, and he knew he said the wrong word. I was the only African American in the building. He turned to me and said, "I am so sorry, Gunny." I told him to forget about it. Being from the place where I grew up, this was not my first time in this situation. He got up and left the table. None of us spoke about this for the rest of the evening.

On Monday morning, the Navy Captain called me into his office. He said to me, "Gunny, I don't know how you keep your composure so well in that situation." He said that the midshipmen who were with us that night, himself included, had found a new level of respect for me. To restrain myself after that incident was amazing to him, and he didn't know if he could have done it. Little did they know I had been in that situation a few times before in my life. I learned from experience that when I find that level of ignorance, I leave it the way I find it. My father always taught me that when you find a fool, leave him a fool because you will not change him. Growing up in Mississippi, any reaction to that kind of ignorance could have cost me my life. Another lesson learned.

During my first few months at the university, I asked Major Ingraham when he thought I should start taking college courses since I noticed he was working on his master's degree. I felt he would be encouraging to me about working on my degree.

He said, "Well, Ike, in about a year, I think you should start working on your degree after you get a feel for things around here."

The following week, I went across town to Columbia College and enrolled in their Criminal Justice program. At the end of the semester, I brought my grades to Major Ingraham and asked if he would include them in my career fitness report. He was pleasantly surprised that I had gotten As in the two courses I took at night. I would continue this for the next three years, taking classes at Columbia College and the University of Missouri. After being at the University of Missouri for about six months, my wife and I bought our first real house. We paid $28,000. This was a significant jump from the $5,000 mobile home we bought while at Parris Island; we were moving on up.

While stationed at the University of Missouri, I

spent six weeks during the summer at Quantico, Virginia, training officer candidates as drill instructors and putting Naval Reserve Officers Training Corps (NROTC) students thru officer boot camp. This program was called the Bulldog Program. College students between their sophomore and junior years of college attended this program during the summer to become Marine Officers when they graduated college. This allowed me to train and meet some of the finest officers for the Marine Corps' future.

As I neared the end of my three-year tour at the university, Major Ingraham was replaced by Major Kahler from Mississippi. We got along great. He was another wonderful mentor, as was Major Ingraham. When I was about three-quarters of the way to finishing my college degree, I applied and asked the Marine Corps to allow me to be a part of a program called the staff Non-Commission Officer's Degree Completion Program. This is a program where the Marine Corps allows enlisted Marines in the rank of E6-E9 to go to college for eighteen months to finish their bachelor's degrees if they have attained sixty credit hours or an associate degree. At the time, I had ninety credit hours toward my degree. I also asked for an extension to stay at the University of Missouri for another year, just in case I did not get selected for the Degree Completion Program.

I was granted a one-year extension, and I was accepted into the degree completion program. The Marine Corps gave me one more bonus. They sent Marine Gunnery Sergeant Frost as my replacement after I had gotten the one-year extension. Frost, his wife, and my family became great friends. They had no children at the time, and they loved spoiling our son Isaac. Major Kahler told me that if I could get my replacement ready to take my place by the end of the summer, I could start school full-time in the fall, six months before my degree completion program would start, and I did.

While at the University of Missouri, my wife Annette worked on campus as a financial aid advisor. In most cases, we could ride to work together every day, drop our son off at daycare, and return home together. Even when I became a full-time student, we would return home together every day except when I started as a full-time college student and student athletics. Yes, I played college basketball.

We got involved in the local church, community, and the university. We met some beautiful people and made great friendships. We are still in contact with some of those people today. We joined the Progressive Baptist Church, where Reverend Butler was our pastor. We grew a lot spiritually. As a student, I also realized one of my childhood goals of playing college basketball. I continued to play intramural sports in the Marine Corps throughout my military career and dreaming about playing college basketball. This dream started during my JV basketball experience in the eighth grade. My basketball skills had gotten improved over the years. After I became a full-time student, while playing pickup games in the gym one day, the coach called me aside and asked me if I was coming out for the basketball team. I was flattered and immediately remembered the dreams I had of playing college basketball. Later that year, I not only went out for the basketball team. I made it and was the starting center for the team.

In December 1982, I graduated with two bachelor's degrees, one in Criminal Justice with honors and psychology. With two bachelor's degrees, I was totally committed to becoming a Marine officer, a goal that I had set early in my career. Before we left the University of Missouri, I requested a MOS job change from the infantry field to the military police field, and it was granted. First, I had to become a Warrant Officer, which was a very tough cut.

In January 1983, I reported to the Military Police headquarters at Camp Lejeune, North Carolina. This is where I met another outstanding officer, Colonel Billy Summerlin, who mentored me. When I checked in, Colonel Summerlin told the Master Gunnery Sergeant to give me my gun and put me on the street because I was a grunt (Infantry) like he was. I was already well trained to be a Cop. The Master Gunnery Sergeant was not impressed with Colonel Summerlin making these comments. So, he took me aside in his office and reminded me that I would go through all the police orientation training just like everyone else. I detected a little jealousy, but I had to get used to it as I would transition from several more MOS before reaching my goal to be a Marine officer.

I had wonderful leaders (Captain Mark Nall and Colonel Billy Summerlin) that mentored me and began to treat me as if I were a fellow officer. At least, that is how I saw it. My peers immediately labeled me as the college-educated Gunnery Sergeant in the unit. This was just my first of many official military specialty job changes in my career. It would be something that I would become accustomed to throughout my career.

Back to Camp Lejeune, North Carolina, 1982

I was assigned as the platoon sergeant for the second police platoon. I had thirty-five Marine policemen and women under my leadership. They all immediately responded to my situational leadership style, and we became the hottest platoon in the department. In less than a year, Colonel Summerlin had a job opening for captain in another department. He called me and told me he was assigning me to this job. I was incredibly grateful because I knew it would add to my pursuit to become a Marine officer. That same year I applied for the Warrant Officer program. I was the number one applicant from the Marine Corps base camp out of two hundred applicants. By pure coincidence, we had a Major from the Military Police department going to Washington DC to sit on the Warrant Officer Selection Board. I felt my chances to be selected getting better and better. Before the Major left for the board in Washington DC., Colonel Summerlin called him into his office with me.

He asked the Major, “Do you know who the number one candidate for Warrant Officer is from Marine Corps Base Camp Lejeune?”

The Major replied, "Yes, sir."

Colonel Summerlin asked, “Who is it?”

The Major answered, "He is sitting right there. It's Gunnery Sergeant Johnson."

Colonel Summerlin replied, "I just wanted to make sure you knew.”

Five weeks passed, and Colonel Summerlin called me at home one night and said, "Big John (that's what he called me), I don't know what the Major is doing up there on that board, but he's telling me you will not be selected." I think Colonel Summerlin was equally disappointed as I was that night. I thanked Colonel Summerlin for his efforts and assured him it would not affect my future performance.

When the Major returned from Washington, his office was down the hall from me but, I noticed he could not look me straight in the face.

Finally, after avoiding me for three weeks, one day, he said, "Gunnery Sergeant Johnson, we need to talk."

I went into his office, and he tried to explain why I didn't get selected for Warrant Officer. He said there was only one slot for the Military Police field. He felt I did not have enough time in the fields, so he selected a staff sergeant who had worked for him in previous years. They were about half as qualified as I was. He continued his story, saying that he did not want to lose me from the Military Police field since Colonel Summerlin liked me so much. The Major could have gotten me selected in another field, but he did not. I thanked him for the feedback, but I knew what had happened. He picked his friend over me.

About three months later, I got orders to go to Iwakuni, Japan. I was a little shocked. Colonel Summerlin was shocked, too. He told me he would get the orders changed so we could have another run at making me a Warrant Officer. I reminded Colonel Summerlin that I had never turned down orders in my career, and I felt I needed to make good on these orders. He tried to explain that I was not needed in Japan because there were other Gunnery Sergeants there not doing police work because there were so many of them there. I told him I would go on anyway, and he gave me his blessings. He reminded me to call him for a recommendation when I got ready to apply for Warrant Officer the following year,

In assessing this short two-year duty station, I had many things to be grateful for. We had an addition to our family, my beautiful baby daughter, Ashli Nicole Johnson. I had another shot at becoming a Warrant Officer. It was my last chance because of the fourteen-year limit. So, we packed up and moved my family halfway around the world to Japan. I was then assigned to Iwakuni, Japan, 1st Marine Corps Air Wing.

Marine Corps Air Station, Iwakuni Japan, 1985

When I got to Iwakuni, Japan, it was just as Colonel Summerlin had explained to me. I did not have a job at the Military Police station. So, I was assigned to Special Services Department. I was given the job as the Special Service Chief, a dead-end position for sure. I was trying to be a Warrant Officer, and I thought that dream was undoubtedly over. Let's see if I can explain what an assignment to the Special Services Department meant to my goal of becoming a Warrant Officer. It was the job given to a Marine whom the unit did not want around doing their real jobs. Do not get me wrong, it was a worthwhile job. Still, I felt I needed to be working in my Military Specialty Job of being a Military Police if I had any chance of getting selected to Warrant Officer. But I was assigned as the Special Service Chief working for GS-12 Civilian, an arrogant and racist white man from Mississippi.

When I first met him, he said, "I am a country boy from Mississippi."

I replied, "I am a country boy from Mississippi, too."

He sat straight up in his chair.

"You are?"

From that day forward, we had a clear understanding of the person we each were. We had many encounters over the next year. He had little to no respect for the Japanese nationals that worked so hard for us in the department, and he would call them derogatory names. I would remind him he could not do things like that. He would reply that he didn't care about any of them.

In the department, we had a combination of Japanese nationals, American civilians, and Marines. Like any other challenge and assignment in the Marine Corps that I had in the past, I took immense pride in this job even though I thought it was a dead-end for my career. I had a talented team of people. We operated the bowling alley, movie theater, golf course, several restaurants, and all the recreational facilities aboard the base. Little did I know, these experiences that I was learning would serve me well in my future jobs.

We arrived in Iwakuni in January 1985. In March 1985, it was time for me to apply for the Warrant Officer program again. This was my last opportunity. I took most of the things in my previous package from Camp Lejeune, put them together, and gave it to the administrative chief, a fellow Gunnery Sergeant. I told him to put it in the same way again. Of course, I had to go through the interview process with my new squadron commander, a lieutenant colonel, and with the base commander, a full colonel.

In my interview with the Squadron Commander,

he asked the question that most folks asked.

"What are you doing with so much education?"

I gave him the answer that my father taught me. I said, "You never know what a man might need in life, so I got what I could."

He reminded me that he had forty Warrant Officer Packages in the squadron and did not typically rank these packages. Still, he felt compelled to rank me number one. I thanked him, but he did not realize that I had been ranked number one at Marine Corps Base Camp Lejeune with over 200 candidates just a year prior. A few days later, I went for my interview with Colonel McCarthy's Base Commander, keeping in mind I had only been on the base for about two months. I did not know any of these senior officers, and they did not know me. Colonel McCarthy called me into his office and told me to sit down and read what he had written for my recommendation. He had written about three sentences, and it read, "Why hasn't this superb candidate been selected already for Warrant Officer? I have commanded Major Marine Corps Installations, and I have never seen a more superior candidate. You can take my word for it; he is qualified to be a captain. The least you can do is make him a Warrant Officer."

I said, "Sir, I want to thank you, but you do not

know me."

He responded, "Johnson, you should have been selected a long time ago."

"But sir, you do not know me."

"I know you. I'm the one that sent you to Special Services to keep an eye on that GS-12 Civilian over there. I know you will keep him straight and take care of my Japanese nationals and all the people there. I already hear that you are doing a great job! Now get back to work."

I thanked him, and I began to feel like a Marine Warrant Officer for the first time. In August of that year, I was selected as a Bulk Fuel Marine Warrant Officer. I was commissioned in January 1986 by Colonel McCarthy.

Iwakuni was a wonderful duty station for my family and me. We lived overseas as a family and experienced a different culture and interacted with the Japanese people. When we were out in the community, our kids were amazing. The Japanese kids and their families would want to touch them to see if they were real. The people were very friendly. They would invite themselves to your home to interact and learn English. We made friends with several Japanese families through the base chapel, where we worshiped.

We also traveled all over Japan—Tokyo, Hiroshima, Fukuoka, Nagasaki, Sasebo, Osaka. We even took the kids to Tokyo Disney World. On Sundays after church, we would drive to Hiroshima because there was a Kentucky Fried Chicken restaurant. We would sometimes go to McDonald's. They both reminded us of home. I was reassigned to Quantico for the Warrant Officer Basic Course for three months while going through The Base School at Quantico and the Bulk Fuel officer's Course at Fort Lee, Virginia, for two months. I moved my family back to Camp Lejeune, North Carolina, where we rented a house off base until I finished my schooling. I would commute home every weekend until I was permanently assigned back to Camp Lejeune.

The Basic School, Marine Corps, Quantico, VA

I began my career as an Infantry Man. I was also a drill instructor at Parris Island and Officer Candidate School, Marine Corps Base Quantico, VA. I completed The Basic School, number nineteen of seventy-five Warrant Officers. Not bad for a thirty-four-year-old. After Basic School, I reported to Fort Lee, Virginia, in Petersburg, VA, to the Quartermaster school for the Bulk Fuel Officer's Course. The Basic School was tough, but my experiences helped to make things better for me. I was there for eight weeks. While at Bulk Fuel School, I became curious about getting an assignment to train Bulk Fuel Marines if I desired to do it later in my career. I enjoyed my time at Fort Lee and thought it would be an excellent place for my family. Another goal that I would set. The Chief Warrant Officer-in-charge explained to me how he was assigned there and told me it was possible that I could be transferred there one day. He did not realize how true his statement was.

Eighth Engineer Support Battalion
Camp Lejeune, North Carolina

I was first assigned as the Bulk Fuel Company's Operation Officer, Eighth Engineer Support Battalion, and Second Force Service Support Group. After about a year as the Operation Officer, my company commander told me that the Commander of the Battalion wanted to see me. I reported to the office and was informed that the adjutant, a Marine captain, had left. He needed someone to fill that job, which included being the legal officer for the battalion. He reminded me that he felt I was qualified, and he hoped I would accept the position as the battalion adjutant and legal officer. I accepted the job.

It was incredibly challenging but rewarding. As the

Battalion Commander was getting to transfer, he called me in. He reminded me of the outstanding job I had done for him. He asked me about my future career goals. I told him I wanted to be a Limited Duty Officer (LDO), which begins at First Lieutenant's rank. I was a Chief Warrant Officer W-2. He asked what he could do to help with that. I explained to him I could not do this as a Bulk Fuel Officer. I needed to complete the required Engineer Maintenance Officer Course to qualify as an Engineer Maintenance Officer for the Battalion. He told me that he would help me get to the school, but it would be up to the next Battalion Commander to give me the Engineer Maintenance Officer's position.

Obtaining this MOS training would make me competitive for selection to LDO 1st Lieutenant. I applied for the course and got accepted. The school was twelve weeks at Marine Corps Base Camp Lejeune, in the courthouse area. The course's approval came from Headquarters Marine Corps. However, the new Battalion Commander told me he did not know if he would let me go because the previous Battalion Commander had spoken so highly of me, and he wanted to see what I could do. I assured him that the Battalion would get along fine without me for a few weeks. A Second Lieutenant administrative officer trained to check into the battalion was my replacement as the Adjunct. I convinced the Battalion Commander that I could have him ready to take my job before I left for school, and I did.

Once in the Engineer Maintenance Officer's course, I prepared myself to be an Engineer Maintenance Management Officer (MMO) for the battalion. I attended the course, along with several of my peers from the same battalion. We had been selected for Warrant Officer on the same board together some years prior. During the last week of the course, the Battalion Commander came to see us, knowing that there was only one engineer maintenance job opening for the battalion, and all of us wanted the job. I felt I might be the last to get it, but I had it on my goal list as one of my objectives to becoming a First Lieutenant LDO.

Just before we graduated, the Battalion Commander came to the school and gave us our assignments. He gave me the job of Engineer Maintenance Officer (MMO). Later that year, I applied for the LDO Program and was accepted and promoted to First Lieutenant. Another goal accomplished. After about a year, I was reassigned as an engineer to the Engineer Support Company for a six-month deployment to Guantánamo Bay, Cuba to support a heavy-equipment platoon. I had some of the most talented Marines I had ever seen. They were mechanics, road graders, bull-doze operators, welders, and truck drivers. Horizontal construction was my new job. I felt like I was back on the farm, moving dirt around. My platoon built the first one-thousand-yard rifle range at Camp Lejeune. During the six-month deployment to Guantánamo Bay, Cuba, we paved the dirt fence line road that separates the American side from the Cuban side. The paving of the road had never been done before.

When I returned from Guantánamo Bay, the Marine Corps policy changed the Limited Duty Officer's Program. This change affected Warrant Officers and Limited Duty Officers in the Engineer Field. It ended the advancement to Limited Duty Officers in the Engineer Field and several other Marine Corps Military Occupational Specialty fields. I had a difficult choice to make. I could stay in the engineering field and not be promoted for the rest of my career or transition to another MOS, continue my promotion opportunities, and grow my career. After much deliberation and counsel, I moved to another field in the Marine Corps. I decide to move to the food service field for a career change. I found myself back at Fort Lee, Virginia, in the Army's food service and commissary course, then back to Camp Lejeune to complete the Marine Corps Food Service Officer Course. I was reassigned to the

1st Marine Division as the 1st Marine Division Food Service Officer, Pendleton, California, in August 1990. Just in time for Desert Shield and Desert Storm.

Desert Storm - A Combat Tour

Combat Tour During Desert Shield/Desert Storm

When Desert Storm began, I was in the process of moving my family to Camp Pendleton, California. When we arrived, we got a room in the temporary housing and waited for permanent housing on base. During that time, I returned to Camp Lejeune to finish the food service senior officer's course. Before I returned to Camp Pendleton, there was a personal message for me from the 1st Marine Division Commanding General saying, get to Saudi Arabia as fast as you can.

My wife and my two children were still in temporary housing, waiting for permanent housing. I had to leave them and get to Saudi Arabia to join my 1st Marine Division. This is when you know you have a battle-tested Marine wife. Annette moved the family across the country, got the house, set it up, and transformed it into a home. When I returned home eight months later from the war, all was well.

When I arrived in Saudi Arabia, I checked in with my staff of two, Gunnery Sergeant Briscoe and Lance Corporal Michael McFarland. I then met my immediate boss. He was a crusty old colonel with thirty-eight years in the Marine Corps and a legend. Colonel J. C. Lilly was his name, and he was the epitome of a Marine leader. Colonel Lily welcomed me and asked what took me so long to get there. He immediately took me in to see General Brigadier General Mike Myatt. They both explained that the division was moving out into the field and needed a feed plan immediately.

I had just gotten out of foodservice school and barely knew what a feed plan was. Still, I assured them that I would have one in a couple of days once I access our foodservice capabilities within the Division. That same night I went to an adjoining camp. I met with the 1st Marine Expeditionary Force higher headquarters' (IMEF) Food Service Officer, Major Nick Shrum. I took his place at the division level, and we later became great friends and confidants.

Nick and I discussed what we needed to do to feed the 1st Marine Division. Nick had been a food service officer for more than twenty years, and I had been one for three months. However, I had been in the Marine Corps for eighteen years. This would be particularly important for me in the future. Major Shrum recommended setting up five 5,000-man mess halls for the 1st Marine Division because we had limited equipment and personnel to get the job done. He explained that many of the commanders prioritized their combat loads in a rush to get to the war and left most of their food service equipment back at Camp Pendleton.

I took his advice under consideration and proceeded to visit all the battalions in the 1st Marine Division. My visit confirmed what Major Shrum told me about the equipment. Before I proceeded, my first order of business was to put my food service staff together. I had an Operation Chief Gunnery Sergeant, Johnnie Briscoe. Johnnie never ceased to amaze me with his knowledge and skill in the food service field. I also had an admin clerk and driver, Lance Corporal Michael McFarland, whom we called Mack. Mack was a young Marine from Tucson, Arizona. He was full of energy and ready to fight. I needed a senior enlisted food service technician because my food tech stayed behind at Camp Pendleton and was not coming because of health concerns. There was only one other Master Gunnery Sergeant E-9 and food technician in the 1st Marine Division. That was Master Gunnery Sergeant Wendell Brown, who was the 11th Marine Regiment's mess manager. I visited his commander, Colonel Patrick Howard, that night. I told him about my situation of not having a food technician for the division. I needed Master Gunnery Sergeant Brown to be the 1st Marine Division food Technician. Colonel Howard immediately agreed with me and consented to let Master Gunnery Sergeant Brown be my food tech. However, Colonel Howard wanted assurances that the 11th Marine Regiment would always be fed well, and I gladly agreed.

My team was formed. I had my staff, and we were ready to work—Food Service Officer First Lieutenant Ike Johnson, Master Gunnery Sgt. Brown, food technician, Operation chief, gunnery Sgt. Johnny Briscoe and my trusted driver and admin man, Lance Corporal Michael McFarland. I returned to the 1st Marine Division Headquarters that night feeling a little better about the situation. However, I didn't know how bad it really was.

The next day we visited every unit in the division, assessing how much equipment and how many cooks they brought to the war. Our count was disappointing. So, my staff and I wrestled with the challenge of following Major Shrum's recommendation on feeding the 1st Marine Division with five 5,000 -man mess halls. It presented a major dilemma. The dilemma was that there was not enough equipment and not enough food service Marines to do the job. We could barely get food, water, fuel, and other resources to one location in the desert, not to mention five locations. My staff and I worked on the feed plan later that night and into the wee hours of the morning with no solution. I told my team to get some rest, and we would resume later that morning.

I went back to my room to get a few hours of sleep. Before I crawled into bed, as I tried to do every night, I read my Bible. The scripture I read in those early hours spoke directly to me. It was Philippians 4:4-6, if I may paraphrase, "Don't worry about anything; instead, pray about everything. Tell God what you need and thank him for all he has done. Then you will experience God's peace, which exceeds anything we can understand. His peace will guard your hearts and minds as you live in Christ Jesus." I went to bed stressed out but somehow knowing that all would be well.

The following day, my team and I met. We developed a feed plan for the makings of the largest field mess hall in Marine Corps history. I asked my team, "What if we take all the cooks in the 1st Marine Division and all the equipment we have and make one large field mess hall?" They quickly replied yes to something they had never seen it done before. Looking for validation for the concept, I asked Master Gunnery Sergeant Brown how they fed the Marines in Vietnam—knowing that he would provide me a great insight on the matter, being a Vietnam Veteran. Master Gunnery Sergeant Brown's answer to me was a classic one.

"Sir, I was a Private First Class E-2 when I was in Vietnam."

I quickly realize this was nothing that this twenty-five-year Marine Vietnam Veteran of food service had ever seen. After we drew up our feed plan and put it on paper, we were convinced that it would work and that it was the only option we had to succeed. My challenge was to convince my bosses, Colonel J. C. Lilly, and Brigadier General Mike Myatt, on my feed plan concept. I made the mistake of sharing my creative plan with Major Shrum, who had given me his feed plan recommendation. My plan was not close to what he recommended.

When he saw my plan, he said, "Ike, if you try to do this, I am going to ask Lieutenant General Boomer to tell Brigadier General Myatt you're a new inexperienced food service officer who doesn't know what he's doing. I can't let you do this."

"Major Shrum, do you have a better plan because the plan you gave me won't work?"

He said, "I am sticking with the plan that I gave you!"

I left his presence and went back and briefed Colonel Lilly and Brigadier General Myatt on the feed plan that I prepared. The feed plan was simple; the field mess hall will provide two hot meals each day, a breakfast and dinner meal with a Meals Ready to Eat packet (MRE) for lunch. However, I explained that I would need every cook in the Division and all the equipment totally under my control.

The first question that Brigadier General Myatt asked me was, “Ike, will this work?”

"Sir, I believe it will, but I also feel that it is our only option. However, Major Shrum doesn’t believe it will work. You may even get a call from Lieutenant General Boomer, telling you I’ve lost my mind have no clue what I'm doing.”

Brigadier General Myatt simply said, “Ike, if you think this will work, I will take care of General Boomer if he calls. But you must sell this to my commanders in the division because these are their Marine cooks and equipment. We are meeting tomorrow morning at 8:30, and you will be first on the agenda.”

Wow! I thought, *What had I gotten myself into?* I went back to my staff and told them that I sold the plan now we must implement it. This would give me operational command of about 600 Food Service Marines and 150 Marine Messmen. We agreed that we could do this, including Lance Corporal Mack. The following day, I met all the commanders of the 1st Marine Division. I laid out the feed plan. The first question that I received after giving them the plan was from one of the Regimental Commanders Colonel, who said, "Ike, let me get this straight. You will provide me with two hot meals each day, breakfast and dinner, and all you want from me are all of my food service Marines and food service equipment brought into the country."

I replied, "Yes, sir."

He said, "I'm in."

Every commander in the room replied, "I'm in."

Brigadier General Myatt and Colonel Lilly gaped at me in disbelief.

Brigadier General Myatt said, "Okay, Ike let's do it."

The next day Colonel Lilly and I drove out into the desert. We selected the area where the 1st Marine Division would operate and where we need to put the field mess. My biggest concern throughout this process was not operating a facility this extensive but getting the necessary support to run the operation correctly. As we looked for a suitable site in the sand, I looked over from where we were, and I saw a small Marine contingency in the distance.

I told Colonel Lilly to drive over to see what was going on over there. To my surprise, it was a group of Marines putting together the makings of the Combat Service Support Division. We introduced ourselves to the commander, Major Kelly. He told us that he was setting up to support the 1st Marine Division. All my engineering experience kicked in again. I told him what I thought the requirements of the mess hall would be in fuel, water, and food supplies. He almost passed out. He assured me that he would do all he could to support me, and from that day forward, this Marine officer was part of my success. Maj. Kelly later became Lieutenant General Kelly, head of installation and logistics for the Marine Corps.

Over the next five days, I gathered all the cooks in the 1st Marine Division and their equipment. We moved into the desert a couple of days ahead of them and put together the first rendition of the largest field mess in the history of the Marine Corps. Brigadier General Myatt instructed his commanders to bring half of the troops to the field, so our first feeding meal was estimated to be about 6000 meals. When the troops got into the desert and gave us the numbers, our first meal was 11,000. We completed that dinner meal. That night, I went to see General Myatt to inform him that his commanders did not leave half of the troops in the rear as he had told them. He was disappointed, but he asked me if we could take care of them. I said, yes, sir, they are there now. From that day forward, the feeding numbers increased drastically. At the height of the war, the 1st Marine Division had over twenty-two battalions in the field. The field mess was feeding over 25,000 meals twice a day. During the war, we relocated the field mess three times as the division moved north into Kuwait. From August 1990 to March 1991, the main subject and priority in the 1st Marine Division was food. General Myatt held a staff meeting every Sunday morning. The main topic was food, and throughout the session, it was about food.

Being the only junior officer on the General's staff at the meeting, commanders would come to me and ask why Brigadier General Myatt was always talking about food. My bosses, Colonel Lilly and General Myatt always came to my defense when commanders would start complaining.

It was nothing for a commander, in the middle of a meeting, to say, "Ike, do you know I had strawberry milk with my cereal this morning? Where's the regular milk?" Or "Ike, when are you going to get some manly cereal?"

I asked, "What's manly cereal, Sir? Cheerios?"

This was followed by laughter. Brigadier General Myatt often pulled me aside in the early days of the war and say, "Ike, there are no Burger Kings out here in the desert; you have got to keep the food coming."

At one Sunday meeting early in the war, one of the commanders complained about how the food looked. I tried to explain to them that I did not control the source of where the food came from and that the pipelines for getting fresh food from America had not been established yet. We were using the local food sources in the area, which was terrible. In the first month of being there, we ate a year's supply of fresh meat in the region. Our buyer had a difficult time finding specific types of food for us. He reached out as far as Greece and other places in the region. However, a lot of the food in the area did not suit the taste of the American palate.

The commanders were getting to me. The General saw this and came to my rescue. He asked the group of commanders if they wanted my job and thought they could do it better. The room went silent. He explained that I was doing the best I could do, and he thought I was doing an outstanding job. He told them to shut the hell up and stop complaining. All the commanders who were not my friends that day became my friend because they knew General Myatt was my friend. After we got our supply lines shipping from the United States, the food got much better.

Later that month, Colonel Lilly told me that the General had recommended me for an accelerated meritorious promotion to the rank of captain. However, before the paperwork could get out of the desert, the war was over, and all battlefield promotions stopped. Still, it was annotated in my fitness report that I had been recommended for accelerated promotion in a combat environment to captain. I was awarded the Bronze Star medal for superior performance in a combat environment.

One of My Worse Days of the War and in the Marine Corps

On Thanksgiving Day 1990, the United States president came to visit the military during Desert Storm. 1st Division's field mess got the dubious pleasure of providing a meal for President Bush, Mrs. Bush, and the other dignitaries that day. A few weeks before that event, a security team came over and briefed us on our roles in this event. My part was simple; prepare about 3500 meals, get them to the 1st Marine Division Headquarters, serve them to the Marines, the president, and his dignitaries on Thanksgiving Day at approximately 2:00 pm.

About a week before the event, I picked up the president's cook. He was responsible for staying with the president's meals from preparation to the president eating the meal. He looked at our field mess and how we cooked, stored, and transported the meals to ensure we were operating correctly. His cook for this mission was a Navy Chief. We became very well acquainted over that week.

On Thanksgiving Day, the Navy Chief and I started about two that morning. We got to the field mess about three, and my staff and I and some 600 cooks and 150 Marine Messman made sure we prepared over 25,000 meals. These were not ordinary meals. This was a Thanksgiving Dinner. A meal that looked like you would have back home in America, and we did it by all measures and standards.

I also coordinated all the American news reporters who wanted to write stories about the Marines eating these meals to report that the Marines had a great Thanksgiving meal. I made sure that reporters from certain parts of the country got to the units that had individual Marines from their area so that they could report on them. We got this done with the help of my team.

After we finished getting out the last 25,000 meals,

we prepared the 3500 meals to be served at the president's event about fifteen to twenty miles northeast of our position. The meals were prepared, and the food containers for the president were marked. This trip was about thirty minutes from the field mess to the General's headquarters on an average day. On this day, it took me over an hour. It felt like every obstacle that could cause a problem for me on this trip did. Every sheepherder in Saudi Arabia crossed my path that day. By the time I got to the site, I discovered that Generals Colin Powell, Norman Schwarzkopf, Lieutenant General Boomer, and General Myatt were also on the list. There were a lot more names, but I will spare you.

They all wanted to know where the Lieutenant is with the food for President Bush. More importantly, will he get here before the President of the United States arrived. We rehearsed the setup plan earlier in the week. The president would:

- Arrive by Helicopter
- Get off and go to the food serving line with the troops
- Eat his meal
- Make his historic speech to the world

I sent Gunnery Sergeant Briscoe, my operation chief, ahead that morning to make sure everything was set up and ready to go, so once we arrived with the food, we could begin serving. We did not anticipate being thirty minutes late. When I arrived, Gunnery Sergeant Briscoe ran to meet me and briefed me that every General there was asking where I was. I had this feeling that my career was dead on arrival, no matter how this turned out.

Once I got on-site, we unloaded the meal and put the food in place. The Camp Commander, a Colonel, approached me. I will not disclose his name. He gave me a piece of his mind.

He asked, "Where in the hell have you been, Lieutenant?"

I said, "Sir, we had problems along the road getting here, and we are running late."

I kept doing what I was doing. Unbeknownst to me, the Colonel was still following me.

He grabbed my shoulder and said, "Dammit, Lieutenant! Tell me where you have been!"

At this point, I knew he was stressing out differently than I was. I turned to him. For the first time in my career, I was about to be very disrespectful to him. But I looked into his eyes and saw the stress. Over his shoulder at a distance, I could see all the generals and dignitaries who gave him hell about my whereabouts. In that second, I knew he needed something to tell them about why I was late.

I said tactfully, "Sir, this morning, we have fed 25,000 Thanksgiving meals to the Marines and Sailors of the 1st Marine Division; These 3500 meals don't mean that much to me. This is just a drop in the bucket. After I'm finished, you can do what you want to me. Now, do you want me to get this set up or not?"

He shrank back and left me alone. I knew I had to tell him something to get the generals off his back, and I needed to get him off my back.

Fortunately for all of us, the president's helicopter was running late. He had not arrived. Our original plan to serve the meal to the president before his speech changed. When President Bush arrived, he went directly to the podium on the back of a truck and gave his address so that all the morning news shows could televise it around the world. After the speech, President Bush, Mrs. Bush, and the generals ate their meals. My team and I fed Generals Colin Powell and Norman Schwarzkopf before on several occasions. They always raved about how well we did the food for our Marines, and this day was no exception. President George H. W. Bush and his wife, staff, and congressional delegation gave wonderful accolades to the 1st Marine Division Food Service Team. It amazed them that they could have a Thanksgiving meal of that quality in the middle of the dessert.

After the event, and all the VIPs were gone, the Colonel, who had previously chewed me out, came to me and said, "Ike, I am so sorry that I came at you like that; but you cannot imagine what was going on."

I told him I understood. He said we got it done. That's what Marines do, and that is all that matters. I agreed. Just like that, I was Ike again and not Lieutenant. We were friends again. That night I spoke with my boss, Colonel Lily, who was not at the event. He told me they had called him three times that day asking where I was.

He said he told them, "He'll be there, don't worry. He's somewhere feeding Marines. That is what he does."

In summary, we designed, developed, operated, and managed the largest field mess in the Marine Corps history in the middle of the desert. At the height of the Desert Shield and Storm war, we move the field mess three times. This field mess fed over 25,000 Marines and Sailors two hot meals each day for several months under combat conditions. Because of this accomplishment, four months into the war, I was recommended for a combat accelerated promotion to captain; and was awarded the Bronze Star medal for superior performance in a combat environment.

In short, I combined all the food of the Food Service Marines in the 1st Marine Division into one unit with all their equipment. This amounted to over four to five hundred Marine cooks and one hundred and fifty Marine mess men. This was the size of the unit that I commanded. This Detachment amounted to over 550 to 600 total Marines for the duration of the war. While working under these adverse and stressful conditions in a combat environment and with the job challenges, I cannot begin to explain the pressures of the job. Before returning home, toward the war's end, I started to develop headaches and have strange dreams at night. Because of the mission requirements and the fact that I could not let my Marine Corps family down at any level, there was no time to be concerned about myself; at least, that is how I saw it. We lost not one Marine. I must give God credit for working through the wonderful team of Marines and especially to my staff, who believed in me unconditionally and worked faithfully to make my vision and leadership a reality. Master Gunnery Sergeant Wendel Brown, Master Sergeant Johnnie Briscoe are now retired. Briscoe had been a Gunnery Sergeant for over ten years. He was promoted the year after the war. Also, Corporal Mack, a great driver, admin man, and friend, was promoted and returned home and to college.

After the war, I returned to Camp Pendleton, California, where my family was waiting with open arms. When I returned home in April 1991, I began to feel a little detached from everything around me. The headaches and dreams continued. I did not want to go out or interact with my family very much. My children notice the change, but my wife covered for me by telling them that daddy was tired. I was depressed and felt guilty about the death of a Warrant Officer friend, Steve Taylor, who was my deputy but was reassigned to the IMEF Food Service at the beginning of the Desert Storm Operation. He was diagnosed with cancer during the war. I knew he was sick, but I didn't realize how bad. When I saw him from time to time, I encouraged him to return home, but he would not think of it; he was a true Marine. I could not convince him to return home to his family until after the war ended. He died a few weeks after I returned home, which added to my depression. I took thirty days of leave to get myself together. After that, I found a new normal to do my job with what we now call PTSD.

My goal was only to spend two years in California, and it worked out exactly that way. From Camp Pendleton, California, we moved back to Parris Island,

South Carolina. My new assignment at Parris Island was the Depot Food Service Officer for the base feeding 5000 Marines three meals per day. This was another dream job for me and a challenge. Going to Parris Island was like returning home from boot camp in 1972 and back in 1976, where I spent two years as a drill instructor. This is the place where we got married and had our first child, Isaac. It was like coming home.

Back to Parris Island, SC For the Third Time

I reported to Parris Island, South Carolina. In July 1996, our son Isaac was going into tenth grade, and Ashli, our daughter, was going into the fourth grade. We reconnected with old friends in the community and began to make new ones. Annette took a job with the Department of Social Services, and we began our new normal.

I have several success stories during my time as the food service officer for the depot at Parris Island. I took the lessons I learned in the desert and set about revamping and streamlining the food services at Parris Island. As Director of Food Service, I managed a budget of over ten million dollars in food and equipment that supported; six mess halls, feeding over 5,000 Marine Recruits three meals daily for four years. I had Marines and civilian employees on staff. My boss was Colonel Hilton, and he had a civilian deputy. Once I got with my staff and food service team, I looked for ways to make things better than I found them, and there were lots of opportunities at Parris Island. We had a food storage warehouse that was scheduled to be replaced. It was old and required a lot of maintenance. In fact, it was scheduled to be replaced in a few years at the cost of $12 million. On any given day, I had $6-8 million worth of food stored there.

One day two people from the Government Accounting Office knocked on my door. They wanted to talk to me about food-service efficiency in the military. They explained they were visiting all the services to see how we felt about buying food from the local economy, like the local restaurants. I told him I thought that it was a great idea. They were surprised I said that. They told me how they had visited all the services, and none of them had my perspective. I explained that the Marine Corps was getting ready to spend $12 million on replacing my food storage facility. We would not need a new food storage facility if we bought food from a local civilian food distribution source and stored it for three to five days in each mess hall.

They wanted to see my food storage facility, so they spent the next day with me as I made my case for this new idea they were pitching for a congressperson who had our third study. When they left, I told him I would like to be the person on the base to test if this became a reality. Three months later, I received a call from my counterpart at Headquarters Marine Corps. They explained that the Government Accounting Office wanted me to test the Prime Vendor program. He asked me if I knew anything about it, and I told him that I had heard about it and would be delighted to do the project.

About two weeks later, I made a trip to Philadelphia, Pennsylvania. The people there explained the tests and talked about all the resources and people they would supply for this test. I was blown away and excited. I returned to Parris Island and readied my staff for this exciting new challenge. Within six months, we had selected a vendor about thirty miles away. We had a new ordering system and started our first deliveries, which was a major success.

To make a long story short, after testing this process for one year, it was hailed as a major success. We celebrated with a signing of a proclamation with all the four services: Army, Navy, Air Force, and Marine Corps. The Undersecretary of Defense for acquisition reform was our guest speaker on this occasion. The Depot Commanding General asked me why I didn't tell him this was a big deal.

I said, "Sir, I have been briefing you for over a year on this project, and yes, it's a big deal."

The military had been storing massive amounts of food in warehouses on bases for over fifty years. This project's success changed the buying and storage of food for all military services. All military branches adopted this new ordering process that changed how the military buy food.

I had another project that I improved on. When the recruits went to the rifle range during their fourth and fifth weeks of training, we provided bagged or boxed lunches prepared by the mess halls. Our consistency with those meals was not particularly good, so now that I had the Prime Vendor program, I asked my vendor to help me solve this problem. The vendor sent me a representative from the Jimmy Dean Food Company. I explained my challenge to the representative. I told him my requirements, and in three weeks, he returned with the beautifully boxed lunch. This boxed lunch was more than I could afford to pay. So, I asked him to take the beautiful wrapping away, put it in a plastic bag, and then give me a new price. The new price met my requirements and my budget. Problem solved, but not the end of the story.

That year the 1996 Olympics were held in Atlanta, Georgia. The Jimmy Dean Company took that box lunch to the Olympics and sold millions of them. When I attended the food show in Chicago the following year, I stopped at a Jimmy Dean booth. You would have thought that I was Jimmy Dean's hero. The Jimmy Dean's reps explained to me, "Captain Johnson, we took that box lunch you created for us to the Olympics, and you made us rich." End of story.

One day, my boss, a colonel, came up with the idea that I should have everything relating to food on the base under my control. I did not argue with him because he was trying to free one of his other captains from the burden of overseeing the commissary store. At the time, he did not know that I had been trained at commissary school at Fort Lee, Virginia, while I was attending the food service course. So, I was ready for the task. I went down and met with the store manager. He explained that we had a renovation project coming up. He showed me all the wonderful things the new commissary renovation would bring to the tune of $4.3 million to improve the old building. He was enormously proud of the upcoming renovation and the changes we would see in our commissary store. I told him I thought it would be a waste of money to put $4 million worth of renovations in such an old building. I asked him if he thought about asking the Defense Commissary Agency (DECA) for a new commissary building. He told me he had not. I told him that I had an idea. It was during the time of Base Realignment and Closure. I told him that the DECA may have a commissary store planned for one of the bases that may be closing, and we may be able to get it. It was just a thought off the top of my head, but I followed up.

When I got back to my office, I called the commissary agency at Fort Lee. I made my case for a new commissary at Parris Island. I explained we were going to spend $4 million on an old building, and they could probably build us a new one for $5 million. The lady on the phone asked me if we would prefer a new commissary, and I said yes. She said she would call me back. In the meantime, I asked my boss to ask the Base General if he wanted a new commissary instead of renovating the old building. He said, yes, if I can get one. We cut the ribbon and opened the new commissary less than eighteen months later. The rest is history.

At Parris Island, I got involved in what the Marine Corps calls the total quality leadership initiative. I went to Little Creek, Virginia, for training and certification, and I trained the senior leadership at Parris Island.

One of the many things that came about from this initiative is defining what we did as a base, creating a clear and succinct mission statement.

When you visit Parris Island and drive down the main street, you will see the three-word mission statement, "We Make Marines." Being a trained specialist in this concept of total quality leadership aided in applying this to my organization as well. We helped Marines and civilian employees identify and understand how they contributed to this mission statement as we did the training. I explained to my class that everyone on the base works toward the goal of making a Marine and is a part of the process.

When I asked my civilian staff if they had ever seen the outcome of what they do at Parris Island, they had no idea what I was talking about or what I was asking. So, I asked if they have ever been to a Recruit Graduation Ceremony. They had not been to a recruit graduation and seemed offended by me asking them the question. Their reply to my question was a loud "No" as if to say why should we go to a Recruit Graduation? I told the entire staff that we would view a Recruit Graduation on the following Friday. What better way to show my team the finished product of their efforts? I had employees working on the base for over twenty-five years who had never seen the results of their work.

I cannot tell you what attending a recruit graduation did for my civilian employees and Marines. Not only were they full of tears of joy, but they had a tremendous amount of gratitude because I thought enough of them to take them to a graduation where they could see the product of their hard work.

My family and I spent four years at Parris Island. There are a lot of great memories. We sent our son Isaac off to college to the University of South Carolina, where he was on the football and golf teams, with a full scholarship, both of which were purely coincidental, but we also planned it. It was coincidental in that it was unlikely that he chose South Carolina State University. It was planned in that we intended he would go to college on an athletic scholarship. When we visited the campus for a black history event, my former boss Major General Clifford Stanley, was the guest speaker. After everyone was gone from campus, Isaac and I took a walk around the campus at the end of the day. While walking, we met an old white gentleman, a janitor who gave us a personal tour of the school. He had keys to everything, and he opened the building for us and showed us various facilities. Isaac was so impressed that on the way home, he made his decision that this is where he would go to school. I later wrote to the president of South Carolina State how this janitor had such an impression my son decided to attend the university and represented the university well.

Isaac started playing golf while in California at the age of twelve. My wife took him and his sister, Ashli, to the golf course every Saturday while I was away in the war. One day, while I was in Saudi Arabia, I picked up a Base Newspaper from Camp Pendleton, and there was a picture of a man holding my son's head as he tried to swing a golf club. The caption read, "Isaac has a baseball swing that he is transitioning to a golf swing." I immediately called home the first chance I got to ask my wife about the picture. She explained that they were in golf lessons every Saturday. When I returned home from the war, my son Isaac and I continued to play golf, and he got better than I could ever think about getting. He also played on his high school golf team, which led to a scholarship at South Carolina State University.

He went out for the football team during his junior year of high school. He wanted to play defensive back. After the first day, he seemed disappointed. On the second day, I did not have to ask how things went at practice. He came to me and said, "You will never guess what happened today. The kid who had the kicking job did not look that good, so I asked the coach to let me try out for the kicker. Now I'm the team kicker dad." Isaac played soccer since he was four years old, and he was known for being the big foot guy, but he did not know that he could kick a football until he tried that day. So, part of his scholarship was also for football at the University of South Carolina.

The next assignment for the Johnson family was to Marine Corps Depot, Quantico, Virginia. I had a short but successful tour at Marine Corps Base Quantico, VA. I arrived in July 1996 and was reassigned November 1997 to The Marine Corps Food Service School, Fort Lee, VA. While at Quantico, I had a great team of Marines and civilians. I implemented the Prime Vendor program there just as I had implemented it at Parris Island, SC. I was also promoted to Major 0-4 while there.

Marine Corps Retirement 1 August 1999

My official retirement date from the United States Marine Corps was August 1, 1999. On July 9, 1999, my retirement ceremony was at The Quartermaster Center for the Army, Fort Lee, Virginia. My staff prepared a wonderful send-off, including a beautiful going away gift. They presented me with a shadow box with the folded American flag flown at the United States Capitol Building, Washington, D. C. on the Fourth of July 1999. The shadow box also had all my medals mounted and the insignia of the ranks I held while in the Marine Corps. I remember that day well. One of my heroes, Major General Clifford Stanley, officiated the occasion. I was deeply moved and thankful that he thought enough of me to come from the West Coast to celebrate the special occasion with my family and me.

Before we took the platform for the retirement ceremony, he warned me how emotionally charged these events could be. He said, Ike, I know you are a tough guy, a former drill instructor, War Hero, etc., but he reminded me that he was there for me. I assured him I would be okay. However, when he began to make his comments about me, he started to choke and tear up. He had to admit to the audience that he shared with me how emotional these types of events could be, and now he was finding himself taking my retirement harder than me.

These were the type of events and situations where friends like Major General Clifford Stanley had endeared and sustained me throughout my life. These were the people who entered my life, helping me realize that I have friends for a lifetime. These were the quality of the friends and leaders that I enjoyed serving and working with during my almost twenty-seven years in the Marine Corps.

Life After the Marine Corps

My First Civilian Job in Twenty-seven Years

I left the Marine Corps in 1999. My family and I retired to the beautiful city of Tallahassee, Florida. I became the Marine Officer Instructor for Leon High School, Marine Corps Junior Reserve Officer Training Corps. This was my dream job after retirement. I spoke it into existence in 1994 while on a recruiting trip at Florida A&M University NROTC Unit. During that visit, I talked with the colonel in charge and asked him if he thought there would ever be a Marine Junior ROTC program in Tallahassee. He replied, "Ike, there are four programs in this town now, two Army, one Air Force, and one Navy. The only school available is the best high school in Tallassee." Retiring to Tallahassee was a dream and a goal ever since I was introduced to college ROTC. I ended the conversation with the Colonel to keep my hopes alive for the future.

Fast forward. Six months later, the Colonel retired and started the Marine Corps Junior ROTC program at Leon High School. When I heard about it, I called him and told him he stole my deal.

He replied, "Ike, I don't know what happened. Leon High School's principal came over one day, and we talked. The next thing I know, I retired and took the job and started the program."

At that point, I told him in no uncertain terms that when I get thirty years in the Marine Corps, I will come for a job. From time to time, I would call the Colonel and check on how things were going and remind him I was coming for my job, and we have a good laugh.

College and High School ROTC programs impressed me so much that I often encouraged retiring Marines to consider serving as an instructor at one of the High School ROTC Programs around the country. In February 1999, I was helping a Lieutenant Colonel friend of mine get qualified for the Marine ROTC program and look for schools around the country where he could work. We were focused on a school in Georgetown, South Carolina. When I got back to my office that day, a thought hit me to check on my job in Tallahassee. I called the Colonel, and we did small talk as usual. Then he said to me, "Ike, you know I'm leaving, and I know you want this job." I was shocked to hear that he was leaving the job. I was in my 27th year in the Marine Corps. I had earlier set a goal that when this job became available and I had completed at least 20 years in the Marine Corps, I would retire and take the job; I did.

You must understand, this job had been on my bucket list and goal sheet before it existed. This was another sign of the power of faith. In that conversation with the Colonel, he informed me that he spoke with someone from Fort Lee a couple of days before we talked. I did not bother to ask him who the person was; I knew it was the Lt. Colonel that I was helping find a retirement job at a Marine Corps Junior ROTC unit in South Carolina. The next day, I spoke with the Lt. Colonel I was helping. I wondered if he would tell me about speaking with the Colonel at Leon High School in Tallahassee. True to his Marine Corps integrity, he told me he talked to the Colonel at Leon in Tallahassee. He went on to say how much he knew I wanted that job, so he had already taken it off his list. I thanked him for that. The next day I proceeded with a plan to leave the Marine Corps for that job. I called the colonel at the high school in Tallahassee and asked him to secure an interview for me for the job. He said he would but advised me that he would not help me in the interview process, nor would he be a part of the interview. Later, I discovered that he was upset with the school about some issue they overruled him on, so he decided to leave the job.

I got the interview set up. On a rainy day in May, I drove to Tallahassee for the interview. I interviewed with a panel-style of several teachers, two assistant principals, and a coach. The interview went well. Afterward, I met with the principal. He was very cordial and thanked me for coming. He reminded me that he had interviewed several full Colonels. I thanked him for the opportunity, and I left.

Less than a week later, I got a phone call from the principal telling me that they wanted me for the job. He reminded me that I was selected ahead of all those full Colonels. I laughed and thanked him. He asked if I could be there by the first of August. There is nothing more humbling than accomplishing goals, answered prayers, and having a grateful heart.

I retired from the Marine Corps and reported to Leon High School on August 1, 1999, in my new role as a civilian high school teacher. I still wore my uniform once a week and as needed. As a friend of mine stated to me at Parris Island, back in 1977, "Being a Naval ROTC instructor at one of the universities around the country, in my opinion, was the best-kept secret in the Marine Corps."

The Marine ROTC curriculum covered the ninth through the twelfth grades. We called our students cadets. I taught most of the classroom instruction along with my deputy, Marine Major Charles Plowman, who managed the administration part of the program. Major Plowman was an outstanding professional and a great friend. We did the drills and physical fitness training together. The Marine Junior ROTC program's mission is to make great citizens. Some cadets would become soldiers, airmen, and sailors, but most will stay home and become great citizens. Even though I was a drill instructor and trained officer candidates, I always ensured that I did not oversell the Marine Corps. I did not oversell because I wanted the cadets who decided to join the Marine Corps to say they joined the Marine Corps because they wanted to be a Marine, not because of Major Johnson.

In this job, I not only knew the cadets, but I knew their parents and families, and I became deeply involved with both. Children do not get to select their parents or choose their environment, and some go through challenging situations. That's why I mentored youth, young Marines, and young adults because many of them had very unpleasant situations growing up. Some of them are still bothered by issues of their childhood into adulthood. We had cadets who lost parents in car accidents, and some parents divorced, and some had other life challenges. I was always concerned and got involved in these students' lives, even to the point that if they joined the Marine Corps and went into combat, I felt personally responsible.

Fast forward to 2003. I took another job at Camp

Lejeune. I received a phone from one of my cadets from Leon High School. This was a nightmare come true.

"Sir, I'm here at Camp Lejeune, and there are several of us here from Tallahassee. We're getting ready to deploy to Iraq."

I contacted each of them to ensure they were emotionally ready for what was ahead of them. To my amazement, they were prepared to go. They all returned home safely from the war and resumed their lives back in the community. Today, one of them holds the rank of Major in the Marine Corps. One is a lawyer in Texas. The others returned and are great citizens with families.

One of my great joys while at Leon High School was that my daughter Ashli and I went to school together every day and came home each evening together. Ashli completed her tenth through twelfth-grade years of school at Leon High School. I remember before we left Fort Lee, Ashli's youth group from church told her they felt sorry for her because her dad would be at the same school. Little did I know, the joke was on me. Two weeks into our first year, Ashli came into my office, asked for money, and said, "Daddy isn't this great! I love it here!" My time at Leon High School was a priceless experience.

We're off to Camp Lejeune, North Carolina; Again

I left Leon High School in the summer of 2002. My wife Annette followed in February 2003. I left with much sorrow and regret because this was my retirement dream job, but I had several more retirement dream jobs on my list. This one lasted two years, but my next goal was to be a business executive. I set this goal when I was back at the University of Missouri when deciding whether to stay in the Marine Corps or get out. I was at the ten-year mark of my career, and businesspeople were offering me jobs. The Missouri highway patrol had accepted me for their next class. My Criminal Justice professor had set that up for me, but I decided to stay in the Marine Corps. However, I did not abandon the dream of working in the business world as an executive for some major corporation.

During my second year at Leon High School, Sodexo-Marriott approached me to help them write the contract to bid on all the Marine Corps food services, which contained fifty-five mess halls on the East and West Coast. During 2001, I would go to Washington DC on my off time and vacation and help them write the contract to provide a civilian food service program for the Marine Corps. After we finished the contract, the company asked me if I would be interested in taking a job with them if they won the contract. I did not see that offer coming, but I said maybe. They asked what it would take. I scribbled a figure on a piece of paper and gave it to them. They did not blink an eye. They said great, and I knew it had to be too low. They won the contract. I got the phone call and the job offer. Long story short, I took a job.

Fortunately for my family and me, I got to work from home in Tallahassee for one year, which gave my daughter Ashli time to graduate high school in May 2002. My original job assignment with Sodexo-Marriott was to be the district manager for Parris Island, with which I was remarkably familiar. However, after the one-year delay in starting the contract with the Marine Corps, the company asked me to be the Vice President for the thirty-two mess halls on the East Coast. The downside was that I had planned to continue to live in Tallahassee. This position meant I must move to Jacksonville, North Carolina, to be in the middle of the East Coast. In the back of my mind, I immediately saw the J. T. Kerr Baptist Church's congregation and the promise that I made to them in 1990 when I left for California that I would be back. God has a sense of humor.

In 2003, after getting Ashli off to college at the University of Northwest Florida, Annette and I moved to Jacksonville, North Carolina. I began my new job as the

Vice President of Operations. I oversaw thirty-two Marine Corps mess halls broken in the three districts. With three district managers all on the East Coast, this was no small task. The startup of this project was brutal. We had to hire new managers and personnel for each mess hall. In some cases, we took over existing contracts, which made things go a little smoother. We got it up and running in October 2002.

In the meantime, I had to play a role in helping to get twenty-two mess halls on the West Coast set up because I was the only person on the company's start-up team with military experience at the executive level. Fortunately for me, I was familiar with most of the retired Marine food service Staff Non-Commission Officers who managed and operated mess halls on the East and West Coast while I was on active duty.

I saw a movie once. It was called "What If Your Dreams Come True." This was the case with my dream of being an executive businessman. For six months, I left home on a Monday morning and returned on Friday night. Do not get me wrong; it was a challenging job but extremely rewarding. I helped provide employment for many retired Marines I served with who were now retired and in the civilian workforce. I made many new friends, and I met a lot of important people.

At the beginning of the Iraq war, fourteen congressmen heard that Sodexho-Marriott was a foreign company. They signed a petition to take the contract from us and give it to an American company. Yes, we were a French-based company, but we were also Sodexho-Marriott USA, an American company. When France chose not to support the United States at the beginning of the war, these congressmen encouraged people to stop eating French fries and call them freedom fries. This is when these congresspeople decide to try to take the contract from Sodexho-Marriott USA. The company asked my boss and me to be the spokespersons for the company. We went to Washington D.C. and went into action to save the contract. We spent time with a Public Relations company that trained us to deal with challenging people in the media, television, radio, business, and interview personnel of all types. Then we were off to Capitol Hill. I was in and out of Senators and Representative Offices for the next two weeks. At the end of two weeks, we won the battle. We won it by threatening to expose something we knew on one of the congressmen leading this senseless fight to cancel the contract. I relearned the lesson that politics is not what you know; it's who you know.

Rebuilding the Village

I borrowed this chapter title from a book by a friend and fellow military man, U. S. Air Force Major General Alfred K. Flowers. "Reflections of a Servant Leader." In his book, he says that the village today as a social-environmental force is missing. He talks about the void that he observed every time he returned to his hometown and hometowns around the country. He spoke about seeing kids from homes where their parents did not stay together, and they don't have loving adults to step up and fill the void. Many kids are struggling and slipping through the cracks by no fault of their own. Many churches are not seeking to fill these voids and miss out on being the stabilizing force that can help unify communities and families.

I retired from public work-life in 2009 but, I continue to help people and work in the community. While in the Marine Corps, I heard leaders ask where these young people come from that are coming into the Marine Corps today. My reply was always the same, Mother America, the village. Over time, I realized the village changed from when I joined the Marine Corps. Two-parent households and family units were no longer the norms. This led me to start a non-profit mentoring organization appropriately named Magnanimous Mentoring to begin the work of re-building the village.

I started by assembling forty to fifty like-minded retired military friends. We were already mentoring about sixty youths at a Community Center. We worked on the reformation and development of young people in our community, one youth at a time. After two weeks, that original number of retired military friends dwindled to the faithful five or six. We started in the low-income part of the community but continued to look for a place to do the best with the resources we had left. We found an opportunity in the county school system with an alternative school for middle and high schoolers who were banished from their home school due to misconduct and sent to the alternative school for rehabilitation. Our mentoring program found its new home and has been there ever since. We are there working with youth to give them a sense of value and purpose.

The principal is like Mother Teresa and a patron saint who sees every student as her baby. Her staff of teachers have hearts of gold. I cannot say enough about this magnanimous team of dedicated volunteers with the same heart. I see this mentoring work as a continuing effort of what most true leaders and I were doing with young Marines and all Marines that crossed our paths while we served. We met with the students every week to help them find a purpose for their lives and show them how to change direction. We used many tools in the process of reformation. The one that I found most helpful was the process of helping them find and see the purpose in what and why they are on planet earth and what they should do now that they are here, and most importantly, how to proceed daily, monthly, quarterly, yearly, three to five years, and beyond.

Every day we ask a student we mentored the questions, "What do you want to Be, Do and Have for yourself and why?" This made sense when they applied this thought process to their lives and situations, and it worked. I taught the concept to my children when they were pre-teens. They didn't like it at first, but they have been benefactors of its successful order. As my children grew up, I had goal-setting meetings with them. They would take out their goal-setting notebook and go over their goals and objectives. We started with their grades then added things they wanted to Be, Do, and Have.

My son Isaac set goals to play golf, be a kicker on his high school and college football team and earn a degree in Hotel Restaurant Management. After high school, Isaac went to South Carolina State University on a football and golf scholarship. Goal accomplished. South Carolina State didn't have the degree that he wanted but, he went there anyway, majoring in business, believing that he could still work in the hotel restaurant management field. There is one thing that I learned with goal setting once the goals are set, it's none of your business how they will be accomplished. You just stay true to the goals and the process.

Two years later, Isaac wanted to be the starting kicker and not just hold the ball and be the second-string kicker. One day Isaac called me from school and told me that he wanted to transfer to a college where he could be the starting placekicker. I told him, let's look around and see what's available. We lived in Quantico, VA, at the time. A few days later, I stopped by the football coach's office at Virginia State University. I told one of the assistant coaches that I had a kicker for him. He asked where he was. I told him at South Carolina State University. I explained that at the end of the school year, we would visit him.

Before I returned home, my phone rang. It was the Virginia State's Head Coach. The rest is history. Isaac transferred to Virginia State and became the starting kicker for the next three years. Virginia State University also had the Hospitality Management degree, which was the original degree that he wanted. However, they did not have a golf team. Because Isaac played golf at South Carolina State University, they allowed him to start a golf team, and the team began competing. I repeat it's none of your business how your goals will be accomplished; you just do the work and follow the process. Isaac set several records at Virginia State University in football as a kicker and as a golfer. I don't have to tell you that Isaac is still a goal setter and shares the concept with his team of hundreds of employees he leads and influences today.

Our daughter, Ashli Nicole, chose the same career field as her brother Isaac. I jokingly say that my kids attended too many conferences at large hotels with me during my career. While on these trips, they would always make a friend with the hotel staff. I would sometimes come out of a session, and I would find them with the desk clerk and other hotel team members learning what they did and how things worked in the hotel. They could always tell me something unique about the hotel where we were staying.

Ashli perfected her goal-setting skills by watching her brother and me. She graduated from the University of Southwest Florida. She is also a Disney world graduate. Ashli has a Master of Science Degree in Hospitality Management and has worked in this industry at all levels. She taught Hospitality Management at Virginia State University, the University of Central Florida, and Georgetown University. Ashli was the Assistant Dean and Director of the campus for the University of Houston, San Antonio, Texas. She is now the CEO and president of her own Hospitality Company in the Atlanta, Georgia, area. In all cases, my children are goal setters. They have learned how to bring things into reality—things they want to Do, Be, and Have.

I shared these same goal-setting concepts with friends, peers, and those I was honored to lead during my career. Today I continue to share this process as a mentor of young people and with you for your continued success from being average to excellent in your life's journey. When I realized I could design, plan, direct, and make my life how I wanted it to be, with my work ethic, abilities, and God-given talents, I was liberated. Now let me share a goal-setting process that I learned and applied to my own life that has helped make the difference between my successes and failures. In his book "Goals," Brian Tracy talks about how to get everything you want faster than you ever thought possible by identifying what you want, making a plan to achieve it, and working on that plan. One of the reasons we fail is that we do not develop new plans when we don't succeed. We must keep trying.

When I learned the power of goal setting many years ago, I had to accept responsibility for my life and everything that happened to me. I had to acknowledge that this life is not a rehearsal for something else. This is the real thing. When I began to study the life of successful people, the acceptance of personal responsibility seemed to be the starting point for most of them. Before that, nothing happens. After we accept responsibility, our whole lives change. I started my discovery of goals without really knowing what I was doing. I sat down and made a list of 129 things I wanted to accomplish in the foreseeable future. As I thought seriously about the list I created and studied it for a few months, my life began to change. Almost every goal on my list started to look like they were doable and achievable in my mind's eyes.

Tracy says, "you can learn anything you need to learn to accomplish any goal you can set for yourself." You must know that you are just as smart as everyone else and that no one is better than you. Everything in life is a learnable skill. Everyone that knows what they know now was weak in that area before they started. Some of today's leaders are in fields that, at one time, they did not know even existed. And what they have done, you can do too.

Here are some thoughts about goal setting that I

learned from Tracy with a bit of practice. Decide exactly what you want in every area of your life. Many people cannot plan their lives past breakfast, but they want the world on their trays. Imagine in your mind's eye that it is possible for you and that you have no limitations. Know that you have all that you need to reach your goal. Take time to write your goals, so you can see them on paper and make them so clear that your mind can see every detail.

Put a timeline on your goals to help you measure where you are along the way in achieving your goals. In other words, make your goals measurable. If you can think and see it clearly in your mind's eye and you are willing to work for it to bring it into existence, you can have it.

Most things are achievable but may not be attainable for you because your goals must be realistic and aligned with your life purpose and the timelines you set for them. There are no unreasonable goals, only unreasonable deadlines. It is crucial to identify the obstacles you must overcome to reach your goal. Know that you may be the biggest obstacle. Remember how I viewed the world from that farm in Mississippi? It was not the farm; it was me. So, start with yourself.

It's always good to identify the knowledge, information, and skills you need to reach your goals. Identify the people whose help you need to accomplish your goal. Make a list of every person in your life you will have to work with or around to achieve your goal. You must have a clear description of what you want to accomplish in every sense. Here are a few big goals that I set for myself and accomplished:

- I wanted a college degree; I have two bachelor's degrees and a master's degree.
- I also wanted a large farm like the one I grew up on; goal accomplished. At one time, I owned 162 acres of land.
- I decided that I wanted a successful military career, I set S.M.A.R.T. goals to accomplish it. I was able to make the most of my 27 years in the Marine Corps.
- I wanted to transition from being an enlisted Marine to a Marine officer midstream in my career; I became a Marine officer.
- I set the goal of becoming a business executive; I was a Vice President in a fortune 500 cooperation.

In all these endeavors and beyond, I used the goal-setting processes to accomplish the goals I set for myself using the simple steps mentioned before to assist me.

Once you have identified the key people whose help you will need, ask yourself this question, "What's in it for them?" The most successful people build and maintain the largest networks of other people they can help and who can help them in return. Always make a list of everything you must do to have to accomplish your goal. "A journey of a thousand miles begins with a single step." You can build the biggest wall in the world, one brick at a time.

Next, organize your list into a plan by arranging the steps you identified by sequence and priority.

- Sequence–what do you have to do before you do something else?
- Priority–what is more important and what is less important?

Organize your plan into steps from the beginning all the way through to the completion of your goal. Select your number one, most important task for each day. Ask yourself if you could only do one thing on the list today, which one activity is most important.

Let me conclude by reminding you that you are unstoppable and can accomplish everything you believe you can. You can BE, DO, and HAVE whatever you want. But you must decide exactly what you want, write it down, plan, and work toward it every day. Do this repeatedly until it becomes a habit, and you will accomplish more in the next few weeks and months than most people accomplish in several years.

Everything I've achieved in my life began with this notion of telling God what I wanted (praying) and believing that He's able and willing to allow me to do it (faith). Next, I planned and set goals then worked until I accomplished them.

Life is guided and orchestrated by the invisible hand of God, moving us all to a life of excellence. God has provided all the resources, people, and places we need to succeed. He gives each person who crosses our path the ability to help us increase our faith and nurture the seed within us so that we can see and move from being "Average to Excellent."

Annette and I Through the Years

My Family

My Son Isaac Me and My Four Grandchildren
Front row: Nathaniel and Karranton,
Back row: Kendall and Lance

My Daughter Ashli, Me
and My Wife Annette

A Life of Service

Lance Corporal Ike Johnson
in Okinawa Japan 1973

1 Lt. Isaiah Johnson

Drill
Instructor
1977

1st Lieutenant Ike Johnson, Master Gunnery Sergeant Wendel Brown, Lt Gen. Boomer, Gunnery Sergeant Johnnie Briscoe and Colonel J. C. Lilly

1st Lt. Ike Johnson and Senator John Glenn
After Desert Storm War

College Basketball Team 1982

Medals and Ribbon Display Presented at My Retirement Ceremony

My Run for NC State Senator

Since my retirement from the Marine Corps, although my uniform has changed, my commitment to being a situational leader and helping people has grown stronger.

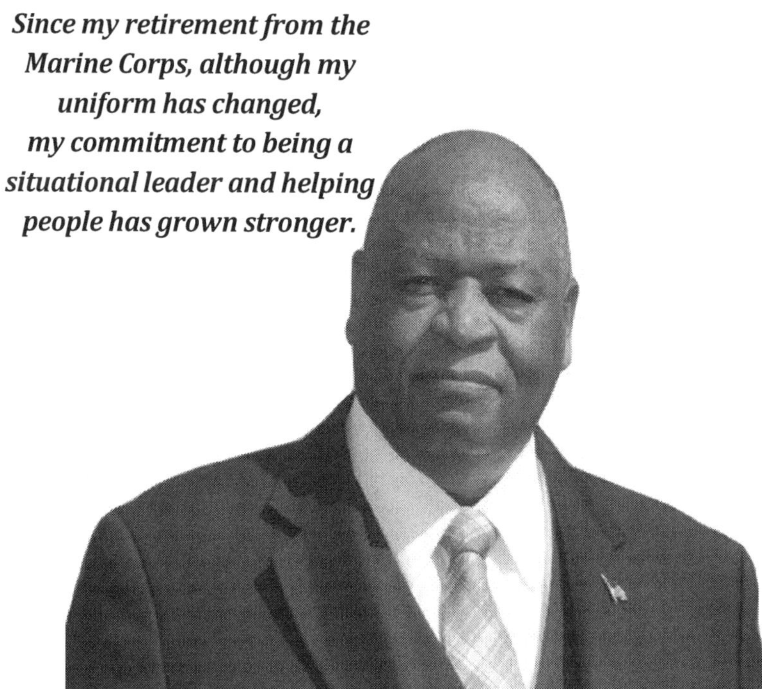

Military Service Summary

Ranks

- Private (E-1)
- Private First Class (E-2)
- Lance Corporal (E-4)
- Sergeant (E-5)
- Staff Sergeant (E-6)
- Gunnery Sergeant (E-7)
- Warrant Officer (W-1) (W-2)
- First Lieutenant (0-2)
- Captain (0-3)
- Major (0-4)

Jobs

- Military Occupational Specialty
- Infantry Machine Gunner
- Infantry Training Instructor
- Drill Instructor
- College Naval Reserve Officer Training Corps Instructor
- Military Policeman
- Bulk Fuel Officer
- Engineer Maintenance Officer
- Food Service Officer

Assignments

- Parris Island SC - Squad Leader in boot Camp and Infantry Training School
- Camp Pendleton CA - Infantry Training Center
- Okinawa Japan - Infantry Squad Leader, 3rd Battalion 4th Marines
- Camp Lejeune, NC - 2nd Battalion 8th Marines, Instructor Infantry Training Center
- Camp Giger, NC - Infantry Training School
- Parris Island, SC - Drill Instructor, 3rd Recruit Battalion, Marine Corps Recruit Depot
- Quantico, VA - Military Drill Instructor, Officer Candidate School
- Columbia, MO - Assistant Military Officer Instructor, University of Missouri
- Camp Lejeune, NC - Military Police Platoon Sergeant, and Director of Support Services Division, Provost Marshall Officer
- Iwakuni Japan - Special Services Chief, Marine Corps, Air Station
- Quantico, VA - Warrant Officer Bulk Fuel Student at the Marine Corps Officer's Basic School
- Fort Lee, VA - Bulk Fuel Quartermaster School Student
- Camp Lejeune, NC - Operation Officer, Bulk Fuel, Company, Adjutant, Eighth Engineer Support Battalion, Student Engineer School, Court House Bay
- Camp Lejeune, NC - Maintenance Management Officer, Support Company; Executive Officer, 8th Engineer Support Battalion

- Fort Lee, VA - Food Service and Commissary Course, Quartermaster School
- Camp Johnson, NC - Senior Course, Food Service School
- Camp Pendleton CA - Food Service Officer 1st Marine Division
- Desert Shield and Desert Storm - Food Service Officer; 1st Marine Division
- Parris Island, SC - Food Service Officer, Marine Corps Recruit Depot
- Quantico, VA - Food Service Officer, Marine Corps Base
- Fort Lee, VA - Commanding Officer of Marine Corps, Food Service School, Quartermaster School

EDUCATION

- Bachelor of Arts Degree, psychology, Columbia College, Columbia, Missouri
- Bachelor of Arts Degree, 1982, Criminal Justice, Columbia College, Columbia, Missouri
- Master of Science Degree, Human Resources Management, Golden Gate University, San Francisco, CA

Personal Military AWARDS

- Bronze Star
- Meritorious Service Medal w/gold star
- Navy Achievement Medal x2
- Good Conduct Medal x4

About the Author

Isaiah (Ike) Johnson has a lifetime of service and a proven history of innovative leadership. Born in rural Mississippi, Ike's early years taught him the values of hard work, looking out for one's neighbors, and giving back to the community. These early lessons set him on a path of service to his country and community that guides his steps today. Ike Johnson is a community resource.

In 1972, Ike enlisted in the United States Marine Corps, beginning a career that would span twenty-seven years. He earned the ranks of Private through Gunnery Sergeant, Warrant Officer One and Two, and then Limited Duty Officer, First Lieutenant to Major. After twenty-seven years of service, Ike Johnson retired at the rank of Major. He is a Desert Strom Combat Veteran who earned a Bronze Star during combat.

He's also a Corporate Executive who managed thirty-two Food Service Marine Corps mess halls and lead employees throughout the East Coast.

As a dedicated family man and serving in the Marine Corps, Ike earned two Bachelor of Arts degrees (Psychology and Criminal Justice) and a Master of Science Degree in Human Resource Management. He is married to Annette Johnson, and they have two children.

Made in the USA
Columbia, SC
08 November 2021

48380051R00080